Jit Samaroo

Panorama 2000: BP Renegades advances to the stage.

RENEGADES

The History of the Renegades Steel Orchestra of Trinidad and Tobago

Hélène Bellour (editor) • Kim Johnson (text) • Milla Riggio (co-editor)
Photography: Jeffrey Chock

MACMILLAN CARIBBEAN

bp
Trinidad and Tobago

Macmillan Education
Between Towns Road, Oxford OX4 3PP
A division of Macmillan Publishers Limited
Companies and representatives throughout the world

www.macmillan-caribbean.com

ISBN 0 333 73311 8 (Pbk)
ISBN 1 4050 0952 7 (Hbk)

First published 2002

Designed by Gary Fielder at AC Design
Illustrated by Tech Type
Cover design by Gary Fielder at AC Design
Cover photograph by Jeffrey Chock
Index compiled by Valerie Chandler

Colour separation by Tenon & Polert Colour Scanning Ltd

Printed and bound in Malaysia

2006 2005 2004 2003 2002
10 9 8 7 6 5 4 3 2 1

Contributing photographers:

Pablo Delano
Arthur Edwards
Lester Forde
Norman Magden

Contributing writers:

Marcia Henville
B. C. Pires
Milla Riggio
Joslynne Carr Sealy

Table of contents

Rehearsal in the panyard. 1997.

Introduction

The unique sound of the steelpan is familiar to people all over the world. At the higher register it is similar to a xylophone but with greater body to it, and more resonance. On the lower bass tones, it is perhaps akin to a large bell, yet less sharp; not clanging but rather booming like a pipe organ.

Individual virtuosos are establishing the instrument firmly in the jazz idiom. Hollywood has popularised it as a motif for things Caribbean, alongside white sand beaches, swaying coconut trees, and folksongs like 'Yellow Bird'. Hundreds of steelbands, as the ensembles of steelpans are called, are scattered throughout Europe. Switzerland can boast of over 120. There are Japanese steelbands and Chinese ones. The University of Alaska has a small steelband, as do hundreds of other American colleges and high schools. Since the 1950s a touring circuit has brought itinerant Trinidadian steelbands to every important concert hall in the world as well as to the more far-flung places, such as Iraq, Malaysia and New Zealand. These touring bands can comprise as few as three or four players, or as many as thirty or forty.

And yet you don't know the full power and glory of the steelpan until you have heard one of the large 120-player steelbands, which are only found in Trinidad. There, in the annual Panorama competition, is the moment of steelband apotheosis, when these vast orchestras release the musical energy which they have worked for months to generate, creating complex tunes and learning them by ear. You have to feel their energy to know it; but it is hoped that this book, through its images and its text, can give a hint to the uninitiated of what they are missing. For those who live in the culture of the steelband, *Renegades* is a celebration of a band which, perhaps more than any other, has come to symbolise the success of steelband music, the BP Renegades Steel Orchestra.

In Trinidad steelbands are more than musical ensembles, and a great steelband is much more than a group of talented percussionists. Perhaps analogous to the samba schools of Rio de Janeiro, the many steelbands of Trinidad and Tobago, well over a hundred, are deeply rooted in the neighbourhoods which they represent and from which they draw new players, administrators, supporters and fans. Every band, some of which may be over half a century old, embodies its unique history in its competitive spirit and in its collective artistry, like a great sporting team combined with a theatre or dance group.

The story of the Renegades is a single but central theme in the overall tapestry of the steelband movement. Other stories tell of the technical elaboration of the instrument, or of the growth and evolution of the ensembles, or the music they created, or indeed of the political unionisation of the movement as a whole. The Renegades narrative is the story of the combativity of the early steelbands, of their bitter internecine feuding and the public condemnation it evoked, and their eventual transcendence. Yet the various stories are all closely related, each one deriving its colour from the other.

The steelband movement was launched by black working-class teenagers in Trinidad during the Second World War when the colonial government banned Carnival. Away from that public glare, these subterranean groups of dustbin drummers and paint-pan beaters sprang up throughout the country, collectively consolidating themselves into an entrenched youth sub-culture. So when VE (Victory in Europe) Day was celebrated as the first post-war Carnival, lo and behold, it was joined by an established steelband movement.

The Trinidad Carnival had always contained a large element of ritualised violence. The nineteenth-century stickfighting carnival bands fought one another with wooden staves, until the practice was put down after the notorious 1881 Canboulay Riots. Thereafter, stickfighting disappeared from the streets, along with the bands of *jamettes,* women whose pleasure was to outrage decent folk. But there were many other expressions of aggression in the masquerade of the masses, which continued well into the twentieth century. Pierrots challenged one another in rhymed erudition and fought with sticks or whips. Pierrot Grenades mocked each other in nonsense verse. Midnight Robbers harangued the public with bombastic rhetoric, and Baby Dolls harassed onlookers with paternity suits. Sailors assaulted people with noise-making bladders while Lucifer's elaborate pantheon of devils, demons, dragons and imps consigned them to eternal damnation. After the chantwells (singers who led the stickfighting gangs) metamorphosed into calypsonians, they too pilloried in song both one another and the establishment.

These rituals had sublimated working-class fury; the iconoclastic steelband movement released it. Indeed, the imperatives of musical orchestration generated tighter bonds within the bands, which in turn amplified the rivalry between them. The result was a raw violence that surprised even its perpetrators. From the late 1940s and through the 1950s, as their art evolved in complexity and each steelband sought to outdo the others musically, they also clashed with bottles and stones, fists and cutlasses. A fight between two men could become a feud between bands that dragged on for years.

Formed in 1945, the band that became known as Renegades quickly became sucked into that territorial gang warfare. Out-manned by the larger steelbands, Renegades survived for over a decade through the fanatical commitment of its members and the determination of some to be as violent as anyone else, and then more so.

The 1960s saw this wave of gang warfare subside, leaving the Renegades beached with an unsavoury reputation. The steelband movement had sublimated the conflict into competition. Music was now the arena for which, as calypsonian David Rudder later put it, panmen sharpened their music blades and sawed off their tenors. Once again the Renegades fell back on their only intrinsic resource: an iron will to defy the odds, to prevail and to triumph. That struggle, however, was to prove far more difficult.

Kim Johnson

II

The project of editing this book was born in the Amoco Renegades panyard during the 1997 Carnival season. Having been invited by the National Carnival Commission to do some research on the Trinidad Carnival in 1996, we came back the following year to spend several months in Trinidad. Our research was focused on masquerade. However, as the season unfolded, the central role that the Panorama competition played in the dynamics of Carnival was too obvious to be ignored. That year the Amoco Renegades dominated the scene. They had won the competition in 1995 and 1996 and they won this time again, becoming the first band ever to achieve three consecutive victories.

Panorama finals, 1997. Photo by Arthur Edwards.

As we witnessed the rehearsals that took place every night for more than eight weeks and shared the excitement generated by the competition, we realised how little was known outside of Trinidad about the origins and unique characteristics of Trinidad steelbands. Among the small number of books written on the subject, only a few have had the opportunity to reach an international audience, and most of them are of a fairly general character. Even in Trinidad the detailed history of a band has never been published in any format larger than a monograph. The story of the Renegades, its present state and tumultuous history, would be of interest, we felt, to Trinidadians and non-Trinidadians alike.

Kim Johnson's articles on pan in the *Trinidad Express* are well known in Trinidad and among steelband specialists abroad. In the last ten years he has systematically interviewed the pioneers who created the steelband movement, not only in Port of Spain but in all parts of the island. As a result his knowledge of the bands and the personalities that shaped them is unsurpassed. His willingness to undertake the task at hand turned this project into a reality. As the work progressed, other contributions were added. We thank Joslynne Carr Sealey, music analyst for Trinidad and Tobago Television, for writing a piece on Jit Samaroo's Panorama arrangements, and journalists Marcia Henville and B.C. Pires for allowing us to use parts of their coverage of the 1996 Amoco Renegades' Panorama rehearsals and performance of 'Pan in a Rage'. We also thank Earl Lovelace, who gave permission to quote an excerpt from his novel *The Dragon Can't Dance.*

Photography in this book is as much part of the narrative as the text. Images of the band in 1997 by Jeffrey Chock, Pablo Delano and Norman Magden provided the first inspiration for the project. Most of the location and archival photography was then provided by Jeffrey Chock, who also helped us define the visual content of the book. Born in Belmont, an area significant to the evolution of Trinidad Carnival, and from a family involved in the preparation of Carnival costumes, he has photographed Carnival for more than twenty years. This made him an ideal collaborator and he closely participated in all aspects of this work. We thank all the photographers who have allowed us to use their photographs, in particular

Panorama preliminaries, 2001.

Arthur Edwards and Lester Forde, as well as Gordon Means and Keith Lohman from Media Production, Northern Illinois University, for their assistance in preparing composites.

Steelbands are very much alive, but as the generation which created the steelband movement is slowly dying out, the story of the movement they created is disappearing with them. It is our hope, then, that this book plays some part in staying the hand of time, by setting down for posterity the record of a remarkable band.

Hélène Bellour, Milla Riggio

Acknowledgements

We thank Renegades' long-time sponsor, BP Trinidad and Tobago (formerly the Trinidad Amoco Oil Company) which supported the initial phase of this project. We are particularly grateful to Frank Arlen, Amoco's Public Relations Officer in 1997, who strongly encouraged us and shared with us his information and his intimate knowledge of the band. The company supported our project with a subsidy that covered part of the costs associated with the production of the manuscript and photographs.

We also thank Jit Samaroo, the band's arranger, for his discreet and constant support and his willingness to let us observe and photograph the band's practice sessions. Michael Marcano, Renegades' chairman, helped us considerably in the early stage of the project. We are also deeply indebted to Andy Duncan, the band's captain (1995–1999), who facilitated our work in every possible way, and to all those past and present Renegades who generously shared with us their time, their memories and their photographs. With their help, completing this book was a pleasure.

Our gratitude to:

Renwick 'Ricko' Alexander, Candice Andrews, Joseph Baird, Beryl Baptiste, Dude Baron, Kelvin 'Pelican' Brown, Winston 'Dr Rat' Bruce, Brian Brumant, Merle Albino de Coteau, Anthony Crichlow, Cecil 'Punch' Cumberbatch, Norman Darway, Wosan Denis, Winston 'Crawl' Downes, Carl Fouche, Leslie-Ann Francis, Hamilton Gabriel, Fitzroy Gadjar, Lionel 'Tanker' George, Stephen Grant, Beverly Gomez-Brown, Karen Granderson, Steve Grant, Cecil 'Dead' Hinkson, Newton 'Mouth' James, Bertrand 'Butch' Kellman, Landeau, Anthony Lewis, Cynthia, Miguel and Lanel Lopez, Anthony 'Castro' McQueen, Oswald McSween, Rupert 'Small Axe' Mader, Gordon Maliphant, Selwyn Mohammed, Kirton 'Eddy Boom' Moore, Harold Moses, Kathy Ann Sample, Lennard 'Boldface' Patrick, Wallace 'Ako' Paul, Nigel Pierre, Raymond 'Brokofoot' Pierre, Hollick Rajkumar, Sonilal Samaroo, Eleanor Thomas, Kenrick Thomas, Nigel Seales, Dawn Songster, Cedric Weekes, Muriel White and Fitz 'Bese' Worrel.

We also thank the Office of Lands and Surveys, the National Archives of Trinidad and Tobago, Melville Brian of Pan Trinbago, Esmond Chapman from the Information Division of the Office of the Prime Minister, *Newsday*, the *Trinidad Express* newspaper, and the *Trinidad Guardian* newspaper, which gave us access to their archives and authorised us to reproduce several of their photographs. The excerpts of songs written by Aldwyn Roberts (Lord Kitchener), Slinger Francisco (Mighty Sparrow) and Carlton Joseph (Lord Blakie) are reproduced in this book through the kind permission of ICE MUSIC LTD. We also thank KK RECORDS for allowing us to use several lines of Lord Laro's 'The Greatest Show on Earth', and David Rudder for his permission to quote excerpts of 'Dus in Yuh Face'. John Cupid of the National Carnival Commission (NCC) first introduced us to Trinidad's rich culture, and the NCC has continued to support our work in more than one way. Finally we owe an indescribable debt to Ronald and Jackie Rose, Gina Humphrey, and Janet Baptiste-John for their hospitality, to Brian Rivas for his generous help in driving us all around Port of Spain, and to Samuel and Laura Kinser, and Tom, Anna and Tommy Riggio, who endured the absences of body and mind that this book so often required. To Samuel Kinser, we are also indebted for his financial support that helped to see this project through some difficult days.

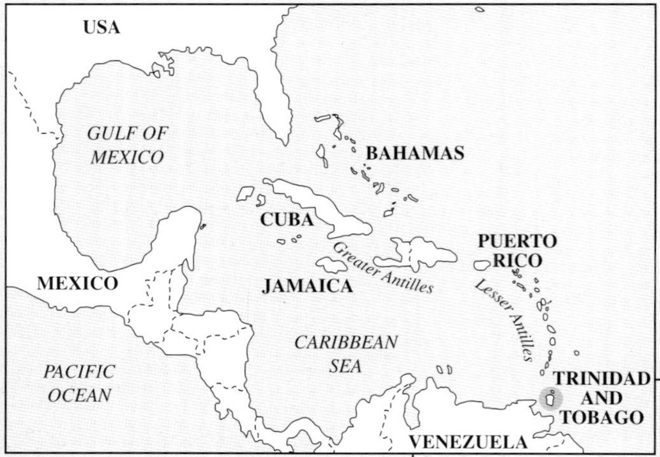

Population
Trinidad: 1,226,285
Trinidad and Tobago: 1,277,675

Size
Trinidad: 4,828 square kilometres

Number of Steelbands
Trinidad: 168
Trinidad and Tobago: 180
Pan around the neck bands,
Trinidad and Tobago: 60

Information communicated
by Pan Trinbago

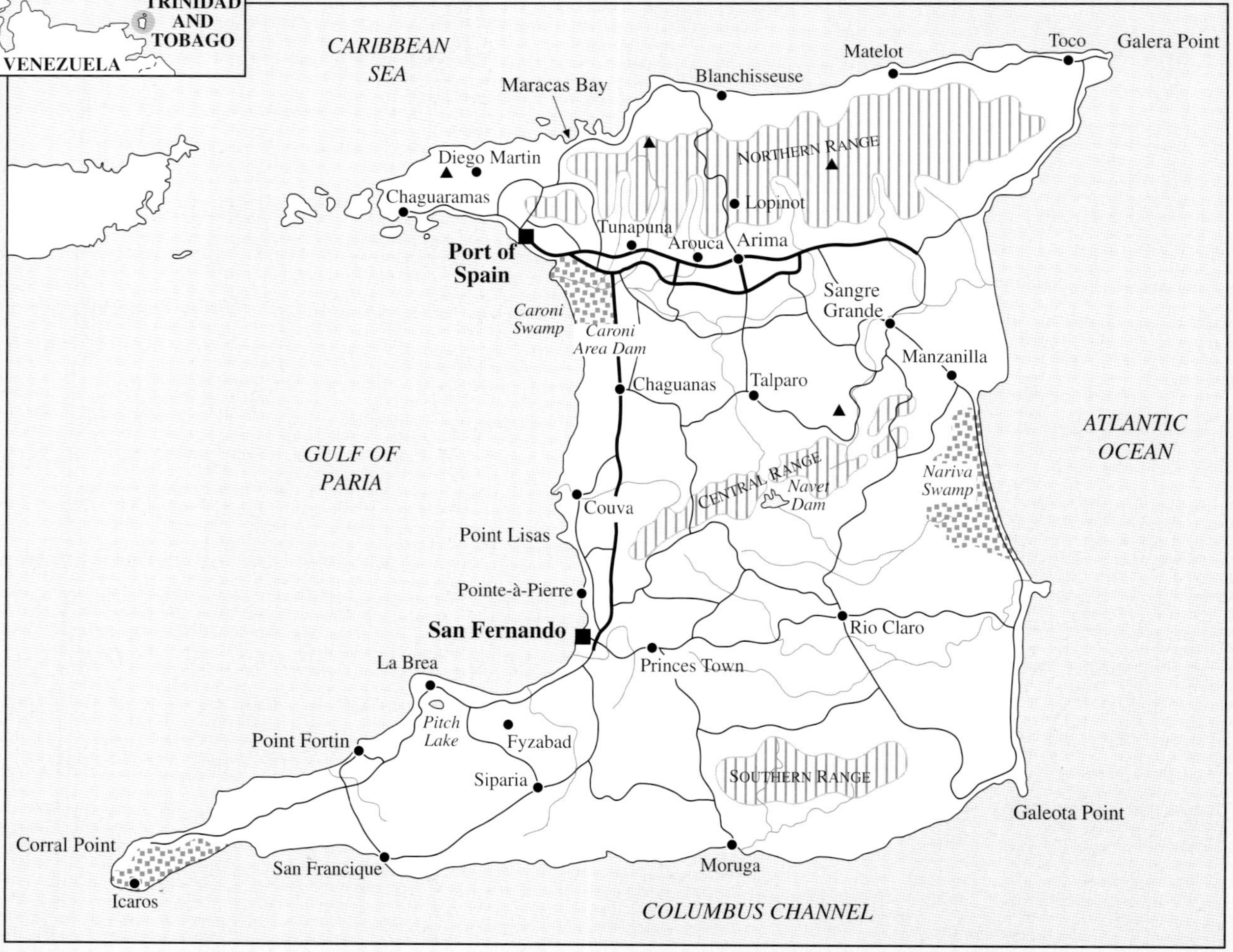

Port of Spain, Calvary Hill, 1997.

Port of Spain

Port of Spain is a city both lively and provincial where restaurants close early but parties last long into the night and the Carnival beat never really dies away. Men and women from all corners of the world landed on these shores: Spanish adventurers and friars, French and British planters and traders, free and enslaved Africans – from Africa, North America and the Caribbean – peons from Venezuela, East Indian indentured workers, Chinese, Portuguese and Syrians, not to mention the Amerindians who first founded the nearby village of Cumucurapo. Trinidad has many small towns and a second city, San Fernando. But Port of Spain is the undisputed urban centre, where the island's Carnival culture and its most celebrated creations – calypso, pan and masquerade – have found their ultimate expression.

Port of Spain, 2000.

A few dates

Preconquest era: Amerindians from the mouth of the Orinoco and neighbouring Caribbean islands settle Trinidad. Archaeological evidence suggests a population of 30,000 on the eve of the conquest.

1498: On his third voyage Columbus sights three hills on the island's south coast and names it Trinidad (Trinity).

1592–1784: For almost two centuries, Trinidad is a sleepy outpost of the Spanish empire. The Amerindian population declines dramatically but remains a presence until the end of the 18th century.

1783: A 'Cedula of Population' invites Catholics to settle in Trinidad for free grants of land, attracting hundreds of planters with their slaves and large numbers of free coloured, some of them planters themselves. The newcomers, who are from the French neighbouring islands, introduce their language and Carnival celebrations.

1797: Trinidad, a Spanish island of French temper, is captured by the British.

1803: The island has over 20,000 African slaves, approximately 2,200 whites, and 5,200 free coloured.

1834–1838: Slavery is abolished. In the next few decades Africans become the dominant presence in Carnival.

1841–1861: About 6,000 Africans rescued from foreign slave ships seized by the British Navy are resettled in Trinidad.

1845: The first of 140,000 indentured workers arrive from India to labour on plantations abandoned by ex-slaves. Immigrants also come from Venezuela, the English-speaking Caribbean islands, Portugal and China. Many languages are spoken, but French Creole ('Patois') prevails among the lower classes.

1881: An attempt to curb the Carnival Canboulay *(cannes brûlées)* torchlit procession sparks rioting. In 1884 the Shiite Muslim festival of Hossein (Hosay) is brutally suppressed in San Fernando.

1897: Trinidad's first labour organisation, the Trinidad Workingmen's Association, is founded.

1898: Norman le Blanc sings the first well-known calypso in English. During the next four decades English replaces French Creole as the common language of the population. Immigration from English-speaking islands continues.

1901: First drilled in 1867 (60 gallons a week), oil is now commercially exploited by a Canadian firm.

1903: A riot against the regime's water policy ends with the burning of the Red House, the seat of the unelected Legislature.

1919: Agitation for higher wages culminates in a successful dockworkers' strike in Port of Spain followed by even more labour unrest throughout the colony. Returning World War I soldiers who suffered racial attacks abroad participate in the action; African nationalist sentiment is a substantial influence, especially in the Port of Spain area.

1922: 'Chieftain' Walter Douglas forms the first commercial calypso revue or tent.

1930–1940: Avant garde artists and writers begin to champion local culture and folklore.

1937: Baptist preacher Tubal Uriah Butler starts a violent oil workers' strike which is quelled by the army, but precipitates the birth of a modern trade union movement.

1939: 'Alexander's Ragtime Band' emerges in Port of Spain on Carnival day with only metal percussion and thus launches the steelband movement.

1945: World War II ends and steelbands dominate the street celebrations

1946: The first general elections are held under universal suffrage.

1956: Eric Williams launches the People's National Movement and wins the elections.

1962: Trinidad and Tobago becomes an independent republic.

Completed in 1848, the Red House has since been the seat of Parliament and, until the late 1970s, the High Court. As such it has been the focus of countless political demonstrations. Razed during the Water Riots of 1903, it was rebuilt in 1907. Its most recent invasion took place in 1990 when Islamic militants held parliamentarians captive in the Red House for five days. Photo 1999.

At the end of the war Trinidad was still a colony. Even now, Central Port of Spain exhibits the British Empire's architecture of power: the Georgian edifices that housed the legislature, the Governor's residence, the assizes. Although the city has turned its back on the sea, the lush northern range gives it a pleasing prospect. Yet visitors in the past have found little in Port of Spain that appealed to the eye.

Patrick Leigh Fermor, an enthusiastic English traveller, soon noticed the liveliness of her people, their uninhibited stylishness, their heterogeneous beauty. After visiting a steelband, the Trinidad All Stars, he compared the city to Byzantium. But he was first disappointed on landing here in 1949:

Queen's Street, Port of Spain, 1997.

The Queen's Park Savannah, formerly a sugar estate, was sold by the Peschier family to the government in 1817. Comprising 232 acres and a three-mile circumference, it is the largest urban park in the Caribbean. In addition to general recreation, kite flying, football, rugby and picnicking, the Savannah was used for club cricket and, until 1996, horse racing. In 1919, at the initiative of the ***Trinidad Guardian*** *newspaper, it was made a location for Carnival competitions. Its pavilion, the Grand Stand, had an upper-class ambience and for decades the downtown venues were more popular with the plebeian masses. By the 1960s, however, the Savannah had become the centre of the festivities, its success being crowned in 1963 by the creation of the Panorama competition. It was a Pyrrhic victory, for that success brought along the hoi polloi that gave 'the big stage' its tone of bacchanal and frenzy. Photo 1998.*

'Dismal barracks and Victorian red-brick public buildings appear, and churches built in servile imitation of the English,' he complained in *The Traveller's Tree*. 'The bleak streets echo with the clatter of trams, and the prevailing weather alternates between damp and debilitating heat … Suburbs and slums trail away for miles. They are replaced here and there by trim white blocks of workers' flats, which are healthy but hideous. Then the slums resume.'

The chaotic settlement on the Laventille hills still contrasts with the neatly planned rectilinear grid of the city's flat land, whose Spanish heritage also holds sway in her numerous parks. In the heart of the city, flanked on two sides by Parliament, the Supreme Court and the National Heritage Library, is Woodford Square, the 'university' at whose 'lectures' Eric Williams launched the nationalist movement, and where knots of men still argue politics, history and criminal cases. But the largest and grandest park is the Queen's Park Savannah to the north, where kites are flown at Easter, dry-season cricket and rainy-season football played, and the Panorama competition staged.

Since Leigh Fermor's visit, much has changed. The barracks no longer exist, having been replaced by low-income apartment blocks. There is now a smattering of uninspired concrete-and-glass high-rise offices in the commercial district. Yet the

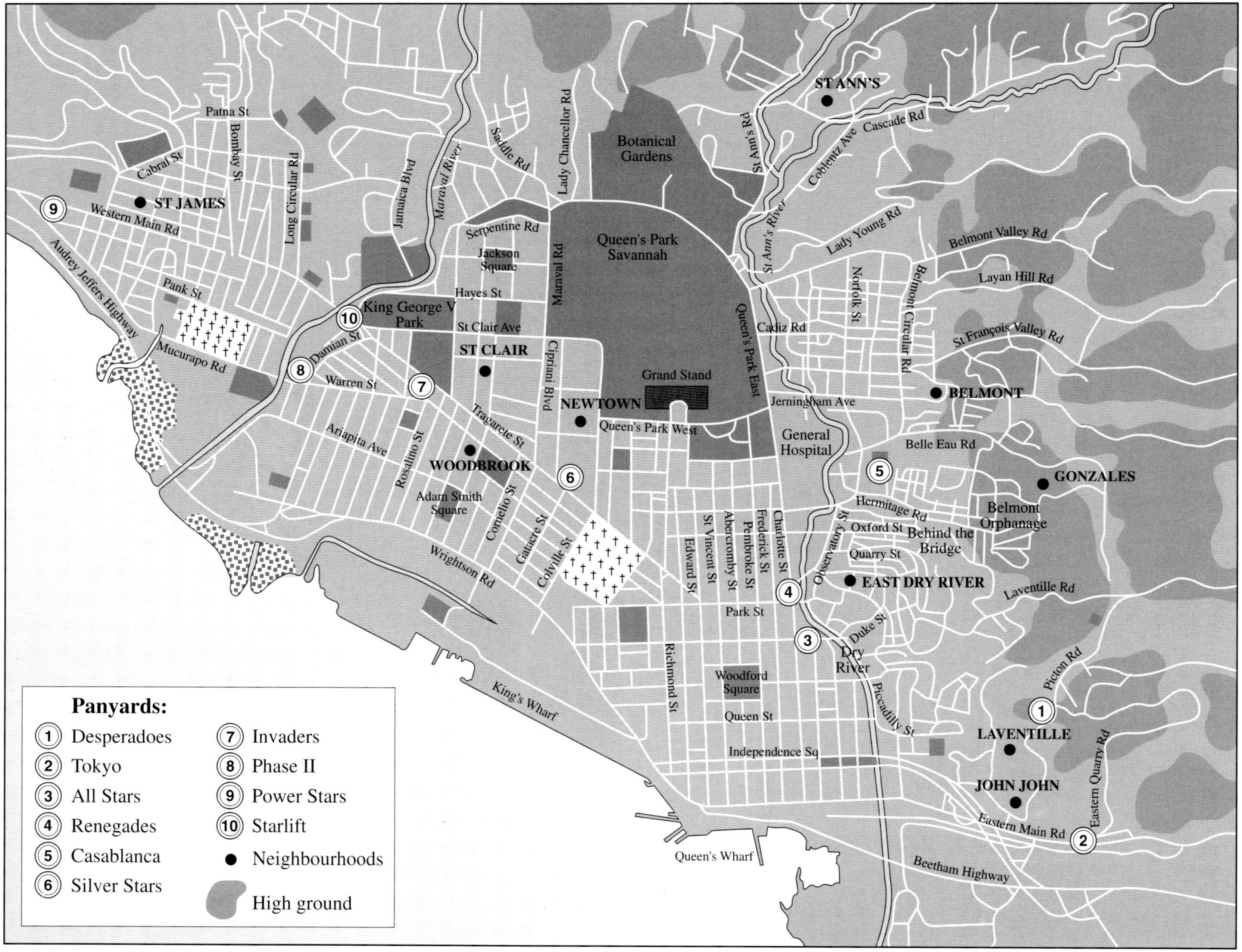

Having a refuge, a place to lime, to practise and to store pans, was critical to a band's survival but most steelbands were itinerant squatters until the 1980s and many still remain such. Pandemonium for instance, a promising Belmont band, collapsed after being evicted from its yard in 1993. The map indicates the panyards' present locations.

Lubin Lane, Renegades' first environment. 1997.

overall architectural tone still derives from an unchanged commercial gracelessness.

In spite of it all, Port of Spain seduces. Nobel Laureate Derek Walcott, in his reluctant 1971 love-letter to the city, observed, 'This ramshackle panache of both architecture and character … has made her seem self-sufficient from tourism … . Being naturally exuberant or so vigorously artificial, she has never had cause to preen her wares, nor reason to isolate then market a single virtue.'

Variety, then, is her virtue. Walk downtown along her main streets, and you will encounter people whose ancestors came from the four corners of the globe: mainly Africa and India, but also a fair sprinkling from Europe, China and the Middle East, and every combination of them all.

Races rub shoulders in the city, and so do classes. In suburban Woodbrook, a staunchly middle-class neighbourhood on her Western flank, lived the working-class men who formed the Invaders.

Steelband in Belmont, Port of Spain, 1998 Carnival season. Small neighbourhood steelbands like this one keep alive the traditional 'pan around the neck' ensembles which pre-date the wheeled racks. Renegades, when it started, would have looked very much like this.

White and coloured Woodbrook shades imperceptibly into respectably working-class St James, itself home for the earliest urbanised Indians, including the Naipaul family. Even in Laventille large concrete houses peer nonchalantly over the rusty zinc roofs of wooden shacks below.

She may not be coarse, but Port of Spain is noisy. From her pavement audiotape vendors you will hear Jamaican reggae and American pop music. At Christmas there is Spanish-Venezuelan *parang*. Throughout her Carnival season live revues blare the latest calypsoes into the cool night. Then there are her large open-air panyards: Renegades fronting upper Charlotte Street, Desperadoes atop The Hill, Laventille Sound Specialists by the Eastern Main Road, Trinidad All Stars tucked beside the Dry River, Tokyo next to the flyover, Invaders opposite the Queen's Park Cricket Club, Phase II hidden in a St James alley, Starlift at the entrance to St James, Hummingbirds Pan Groove at its exit.

Driving through the city after dark you first hear some band's iron gently ringing from afar like a metronome with swing. As you approach the panyard the rumble of the bass is seeping out, and the tenors' melody rides the breeze like a soft whistle. Close up, of course, all is orchestral thunder and lightning.

'Port of Spain is a tolerant, cosmopolitan, relatively well-educated city,' summed up James Morris, another English traveller who visited the island in the 1950s. 'But one sometimes feels that for all the [cricket] stroke-play and the intelligence the real essence of the place is contained in these raw and raucous celebrations.'

1

Genesis

I had a dream last night in my cacheau
An angel came down and whisper
Kitch, is time to get Hitler.
I hope the government would now agree
And send the steelband from John John to Germany.
Hear they singing
Adolf Hitler, here come your enemy.
We are quite prepared to meet this madman from Germany.
No bullets, no gun
The beating of the steelband go make you run
Adolf Hitler be on your guard
Here come the steelband from Trinidad.

(Lord Kitchener 'A Dream in my Cacheau')
Courtesy of Ice Music

Halfway up Basilon Street, 1997.

Behind the bridge...

When it all began at the end of the forties, Basilon Street was one of the many narrow passages that curved steeply into the foothills of Laventille, East Port of Spain. Here the mostly black working class built their tiny houses and shacks cheek by jowl but in no particular order. Privacy hardly existed in these quarters. Life was lived outdoors where children played, men gambled and women gossiped. To outsiders it was a rough, forbidding area, but those living around Basilon Street had their own sense of propriety and shared a keen sense of belonging, as did the inhabitants of each of the countless tiny districts that made up the large community of Laventille. Here it was that the Renegades Steel Orchestra was born on Empire Day, 24 May 1948.

Atop Lubin Lane, by Calvary Hill, 1997.

Behind the bridge. East Dry River. Laventille. There are other poor black districts in and around Port of Spain, but the steep hills east of the city, and the tight community they spawned, embody the heart of the city's Afro-Trinidadian plebeian culture. The St Ann's river, a brown trickle in its paved canal, could be as wide as the River Jordan for the worlds it separates. West, the city's grid sprawls its anarchy of colours and races and classes; east, the rocky hills of Laventille perch, almost uniformly black and poor, with narrow winding roads and a maze of steep lanes through which a car could not squeeze. They are re-paved now, and often fronted by large houses belonging to ambitious, respectable families. But in the fifties the uppermost streets were often dirt or mud. Addresses were rare. To find a house it was nothing to have to first balance along the edge of a gutter, clamber over some rocks, and then walk through somebody's yard and around a latrine.

The East Dry River's flatlands were simply working class, but further into Laventille's nether reaches there were people who invaded the city solely at Carnival. Squatted in the nineteenth century by ex-slaves, the hill's steep forests were considered beyond civilisation's reach, culturally and administratively, and the area was left to develop according to its own logic. The twentieth century brought massive quarrying operations which sharpened the hill's already rugged, forbidding contours; and massive immigration, often illegal, from other islands, heightened its sense of otherness.

Outsiders did not set foot east of the Dry River. Even working-class people from other districts steered clear of Laventille. Only the police entered, and then in their numbers like an invading army in search of felons or a marauding steelband. But impassive eyes met their passage as the labyrinthine roads defeated them.

The East Dry River, 1997.

This modern Carnival Monday (J'ouvert) scene, 1996, recreates the tamboo bamboo at its late 1930s moment of transition. The mid-range bamboo fuller is accompanied by a two-note 'du dup' or 'bass kettle', made from a modern 35-gallon drum, and a scratcher or scraper.

Origins

By the end of the war there had long been steelbands throughout Trinidad, scores of them. They had first seen the light of day in 1939 and within months new ones sprouted wherever there were groups of black youth. Renegades were relative newcomers. But in one sense they were not, for the band had a genealogy that reached back even before the steelband was invented, back to the tamboo bamboo percussion ensembles of the thirties.

In the beginning was the drum.

Africans brought music and dance, their quintessential arts, to the New World plantations. Music and dance provided solace and celebration; they lightened the slaves' earthly burdens and invoked their African gods. Here the drum was central. In many territories drums were banned, out of a fear for their power to incite and communicate servile rebellion but also because their throbbing pulse was awful to European ears.

Nevertheless, in Trinidad the drum dances persisted, and once slavery was abolished in 1838 the freed Africans carried them on through the Christmas and Carnival seasons, to the revulsion of the French and English upper class. Laws restricted the hours when drum dances could be held; property owners were fined for allowing them on their premises. Still the noisy revelry continued in slums and in the mountain fastness where policemen feared to tread. And for Carnival, starting with the Sunday night torchlit processions known as Canboulay (from the French: *cannes brûlées*), the revelry invaded the city in the form of black people in 'obscene' costumes, yelling scandalous songs, performing 'lewd' dances and pounding fearful drums.

The nineteenth century was a time of fracture. The white upper class was divided between Catholics and Anglicans, between the French and the English. Thousands of labourers were landing annually from India for the sugar plantations. There were also peons from Venezuela in the cocoa highlands, and Chinese and Portuguese shopkeepers in every small town or village. Amongst the black majority population, Trinidad Creoles jostled for space in a crowded city, for jobs in the deepening economic recession, for a sense of identity, against Barbadians, Grenadians, Vincentians, Martiniquans, 'Merikins' and other immigrants. Tribal links surfaced: Rada, Mandingo, Yoruba, Congo. As freedom compelled this deeply fissured society to confront itself, the conflict and incomprehension, the rivalry and resentment found expression and sublimation in Carnival.

Lithograph of Barbados slaves stickfighting, by A. Brunias, 1779. Stickfighting accompanied by drumming was practised by the African diaspora in many areas of the New World. In nineteenth-century Trinidad this martial sport associated with a drum dance, the 'calinda', was the act of marauding gangs as well as individual exponents. East Indians also had a form of stickfighting called 'gatka'.

'There appear to be about a dozen different bands, each generally representing young vagabonds and semi-vagabonds of a street or locale,' observed the *Trinidad Chronicle* on 9 February 1877. These neighbourhood gangs were led by chantwells who sang simple ditties to which the crowd provided a choral response, and they roamed Port of Spain during Carnival, singing, drumming and looking for rivals to fight. The weapon of choice was the *bois* – a three-foot hardwood staff often 'mounted', i.e. prepared with magic to ensure invulnerability. Thus stickfighting, a traditional West African martial sport performed to drums and chants, became a main channel of plebeian rage. But when bands clashed, *bois* often gave way to bottles, and sticks were replaced by stones, in an all-out free-for-all.

Strenuous police efforts to clean up the Carnival precipitated major riots in 1881 and 1884, but eventually the drum dances were suppressed in the city. The gangs dispersed and thereafter stickfighting became more a matter of individual prowess, rather than community ascendancy.

Drums were replaced by tamboo bamboo – ensembles that used hollow bamboo stalks for percussion, stamping them on the ground or knocking them together to provide syncopated rhythms for masqueraders, stickfighters and rustic calypsonians.

A 1920 newspaper report (*Trinidad Guardian*, 5 February 1920) described one such performance:

> It began with the booming sound of the bass bamboo which serves to regulate the time, and after a few beats, a number of the band who played the lighter reeds joined in. The 'cutting' (beating) of the finer reeds in rhythmic punctuation between the boom of the bass bamboo was really surprising. The Shac Shac player and the bottle and spoon operators completed the orchestra, and the music was furnished by the chanting of a 'single re' by the director in a high-pitched tenor, and then taken up in chorus by other members of the band, not excluding the orchestra ...

From the mid-thirties metal entered the tamboo bamboo, starting with the large biscuit drum 'cuff boom', which was thumped on its base with the fist. 'It also used to have a man walking backwards in front the cuff boom cutting [syncopating] on it', recalls Joseph Baird, a founding member of Renegades, describing the small tamboo bamboo band that came from Basilon Street. 'Pelican' [Pelican Brown, another founding member] as a baby used to do that – we had to hold him to cut.'

The group Baird was referring to, led by a certain Lennus Simms, was one of the numerous bands combining metal percussion and bamboos

The drummer here plays a bass drum. Laws in the 1880s forbade such drums in the streets, and severely restricted drum dances. Tamboo bamboo was substituted for Carnival activities, but in African religious ceremonies drumming persisted throughout the countryside and the hills around Port of Spain.

African drum ensembles often come in threes, which translated into the three sections of tamboo bamboo bands – the 'bass', the 'fuller' and the 'cutter'. Later they became the background, mid-range and lead sections of the steelband. There was also a fourth voice, however, which was higher, more insistent. Manifest in the tamboo bamboo as a gin bottle and spoon, it evolved into the iron in the steelband, which in turn expanded into the rhythm section known as the engine room.

While extensive use of metal percussion began only in the 1930s, metal objects had been used for percussion since the mid-nineteeth century. The background photograph shows a masquerader performing to the percussive rhythm of a biscuit tin. Cavorting to tattoos drummed on a recycled container, such 'Jab molassie' (Molasses Devils, now smeared with grease rather than molasses) still terrorise Carnival onlookers.

This postcard, circa 1940, shows an unidentified prototype steelband. The bass drum, which originally contained biscuits, was called the 'cuff boom'. Note the man walking backwards and syncopating on its side. Photo circa 1940, probably at Carnival in Port of Spain.

in the years before the Second World War. By 1939 a few bands had evolved or were evolving into all-metal ensembles. One of these groups, calling itself Alexander's Ragtime Band, made a spectacular appearance on Carnival Monday, drumming exclusively on pots and pans, dustbins and scraps of derelict cars – the detritus of modern industrial civilisation. Thus was publicly launched the steelband movement. Those pots and pans and dustbins produced only noisy rhythms, but there was something about it – perhaps its harsh volume, its virile metallic tones – that seemed appropriate to modern times (the electric guitar was invented only a few years later, in 1948), and the embryonic steelband movement immediately made tamboo bamboo redundant. The older tamboo bamboo men quietly withdrew and a younger, more assertive generation took over.

Shortly afterwards, the Second World War intervened. Port of Spain was lively during the war. A large American military base on the island's north-western peninsula provided well-paid employment as never seen before for tens of thousands in the island. The entertainment industry in particular, both licit and illicit, which catered for the rich bored US servicemen, boomed. 'Mother and daughter working for the Yankee dollar', sang the calypsonian Lord Invader in 'Rum and Coca Cola' – a calypso plagiarised in the US by the Andrews Sisters, who never realised its sexual connotation.

Still, those years were hard. Food was rationed, as were car tyres and gasoline. Blackouts were enforced. Public meetings and processions were rigorously prohibited. From 1942, Carnival, the festival which had given birth to steelbands, was banned.

These were the years when the first few notes were put on pans. Young men were forming metal percussion groups throughout the island, cocooned in empty lots or under the houses of indulgent parents, experimenting. In Port of Spain the bands, flushed with the excitement of their recent creation, paraded in defiance of the wartime ban, hiding in the Laventille's labyrinthine passages, waging a guerrilla war with the police who attempted to quell the music. But that cat and mouse game was frustrating, so when the government promised a holiday on the signing of peace, feverish preparations were begun to celebrate.

'For weeks on end the boys of "Hell Yard," "Gonzales," Belmont, "Bar 20," New Town, John John, St James, La Cour Harp, "Men of Boys Town" and Rose Hill had been occasionally "warming up" in backyards waiting for ANY Carnival Day,' described reporter Brunell Jones ('V-E Day, What a DAY!' in *Sport and Music Cavalcade* Vol. 1, No. 3, p.101). So when the war ended on 8 May 1945 – VE (Victory in Europe) Day – and the society felt again its need for music in the streets, steelbands emerged from every Afro-Trinidadian neighbourhood – including Basilon Street, the birthplace of the Renegades – and a joyful clanging, banging tintinnabulation filled the streets of Port of Spain.

The Basilon Street district already had a steelband: Bar 20 had been formed five years before in a Bath Street brothel at the bottom of Basilon Street. Unfortunately, that band harboured some of the city's most disreputable characters, pimps and streetfighters, men boasting long criminal records. Yvonne 'Bubulups' Smith, one of the women who flew their skull-and-crossbones flag, was the most infamous prostitute in the country.

'The Bar 20 fellas was fellas who [were] gambling, they make prison,' recalls Joseph Baird, who was a Basilon Street teenager during the war. 'Our parents didn't want us associate with them so we had to take a chance to jump with them. We decided to open our own band around there. Ethelbert Serrette decided it. He did everything at the beginning. He get us together.'

The Ohio Casanovas

Serrette, a joiner by trade, had played in the Basilon Street's pre-war tamboo bamboo band. He was slightly older than the 18-year-old Baird, but they were friends. Along with several of the other young men from the neighbourhood, they had formed the Ohio Sports Club to play cricket and football, to box and wrestle and lift weights. At nights, stylishly dressed, they went as a group to dances, calling themselves the Casanovas. Once a year they also held a dance that was attended by young and old alike from the district.

'Black Legion', formerly 'Midnight Tollers'. Courtesy of Dude Baron. This band came from Basilon Street on Carnival Tuesday, 1946. Lionel Brown is on the left while his son, Kelvin 'Pelican' Brown, peeps above the banner.

Midnight Robbers often prowled in small groups but competed as individuals against rivals, using grandiloquent, boastful speeches of their feats and fearsomeness.

Like many other such groups they wanted a steelband with which to parade the streets on VE Day and VJ (Victory over Japan) Day, and more so on the first Carnival after the war, in 1946. Steelbands were rudimentary affairs, only capable of simple tunes and nursery rhymes and a loud banging rhythm, but already they were an obsession amongst young Afro-Trinidadians. Serrette foraged pans from wherever he could, asking other bands, particularly Bar 20. He also pulled in some of the younger boys of the district because, after all, when it was time to dance, the Casanovas would not want to be burdened with having to play music.

'You see how you get a group to form a band?' explains Baird. 'When 'Telbert form it it had no name, only a flourbag flag with a skull and crossbones on it. The senior citizens joined in the band with us. They knew everybody, a set of mothers and aunts. When we was beating [pan] in the road people would say, "Look Ohio band" because they recognised the members of the sports club.'

In 1946 the Ohio Casanovas, as the band was called, played early on the Monday morning of that first Carnival after the war. Later that day they put aside their pans and joined the Black Legion, a band of Midnight Robber masqueraders organised by Lionel 'Two-Gun Crawley' Brown, the father of Ohio panman Kelvin 'Pelican' Brown. The steelband played on the roads that night and again the following day when they wore Red Indian costumes provided by Serrette.

Joseph Baird shows the place where the decision was made to rebuild the band after Serrette's rampage.

The next year, 1947, the steelband started off with the same itinerary, playing on the morning and night of Carnival Monday. For the Tuesday, however, the proprietary Serrette had other plans. He instructed the boys to leave the pans at his house where they were usually stored. But since the band had been formed, steelband had changed: lead 'ping pong' pans had up to a dozen notes, the music now demanded greater commitment. It also evoked greater passions. Panmen could not put their pans aside on Carnival Tuesday just because of one man's whim, so the minute Serrette turned his back the youths took them and went playing on the streets.

Somehow Serrette found out. He collected a hatchet from home and went looking for them. When he spotted the band about a mile away on New Street, uptown Port of Spain, he attacked. Whoever was able to run with their instrument did so, the others dropped theirs and fled in disarray, and Serrette destroyed every pan on which he got his hands.

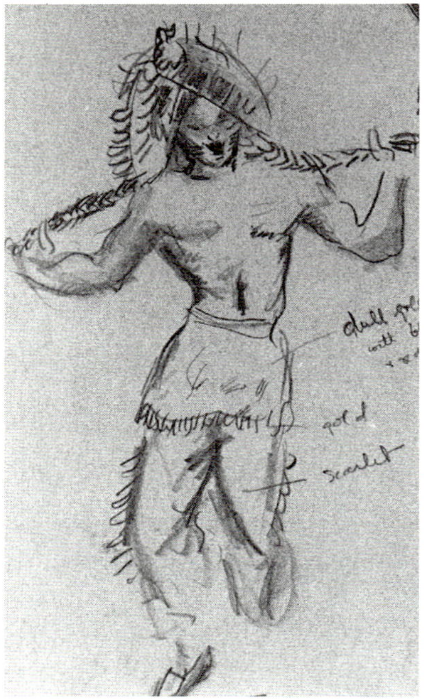

Indian masker by Carlisle Chang. Indian mas in the 1950s could be Red, Black, White, Wild or Fancy. Some Indians wore elaborate costumes, but some Indian mas was simple, inexpensive and very popular in lower-class neighbourhoods. Indians moved in fierce or ornate-looking tribes, often challenging rival bands to banter in an invented language. Courtesy of Carlisle Chang.

For the first time, but not the last, the band that later became famous as the Renegades contemplated extinction. But on Ash Wednesday the players, most of whom were no older than fourteen or fifteen, met and decided to regroup. They were joined by several new members, youths who had been hanging around older bands but wanted their own. These included Lionel 'Tanker' George, Carlton Clarke and Alvin 'Yankee Boy' George, who in spite of his youth was a gifted tuner who could fabricate instruments for an entire band in a day, whistling all the while.

From Pelican Brown's father, the foreman at a quarry located in Basilon Street, they got permission to store their pans in an unused kiln. Then there was another infusion of members from another small band, East Side Kids, based in the adjoining district of La Cour Harpe. There were even fewer of these but they forged a link between Basilon Street and La Cour Harpe, a bond that would endure through thick and thin until, years later, Harpe residents constituted the backbone of the band and shaped its personality.

VJ (Victory in Japan) Day, August 1945, Port of Spain. Courtesy of Dude Baron.

The road make to walk on Carnival day

Taking over the roads ***en masse*** in Trinidad has long been a symbol for claiming the land. To the former slaves emancipated in 1838, it was the privilege of the free, a gesture of liberation perhaps similar to what mounting the barricades meant to Parisians.

The late nineteenth-century battles in Trinidad between the upper and lower classes were fought over this issue. The Canboulay processions which filled Port of Spain with drunken stickfighters on Carnival Sunday night, and the Hosay processions which filled San Fernando with East-Indians both terrified the ruling class.

To black Trinidadians, Carnival was a powerful symbol, a moment when they affirmed and celebrated the many dimensions of their African heritage: in dance, in costume, in song, in words and in percussion.

No wonder the history of Carnival has been one long struggle over who would control the streets, a battle that was fought again and won by the steelbands, albeit at great cost. Panmen fought their family and friends and the police, and they expanded that freedom. They paraded the streets on public holidays, in the Christmas season, or whenever the mood took them, fleeing when necessary from the slow arm of the law.

Carnival Monday morning (J'ouvert) 1996.

From steeldrums to steel orchestra

Members of the Laventille Rhythm Section, Carnival, 1996. The pan in front is a two-note 'du dup' made from a present-day drum; right behind it the 'iron' – originally an automobile brake drum – dominates the band's rhythm. Note the man to the right holding a cowbell.

Steelband instruments

The rhythm in the band

At the creation of the Ohio Casanovas, steelbands were essentially rhythm makers. At Carnival people chanted their melodies to the booming and clanging of the pans. Barring regional variations, steelbands had five different instruments.

The loudest, most primitive and yet the most enduring instrument in those early ensembles was the *iron* – a brake hub from a car, although one band had a truck's brake hub, whose player stuffed his ears and carried it on his head. The iron was drummed with a pencil-sized steel rod, and sounded like a cowbell with more ring to it. The iron is still a vital component in a steelband.

For the bass (background) section there was the biscuit drum or *boom*. A large, broad drum of lightweight steel, it was strapped horizontally in front of the player who thumped its face with his fist to produce a constant deep pulse: *boom, boom, boom.*

Also in the background section was the *tenor boom* or *du dup*. Slung diagonally across the hip, this contributed the two-note beat that gave it its name: *du-dup, dip, dup; du-dup, dip, dup.*

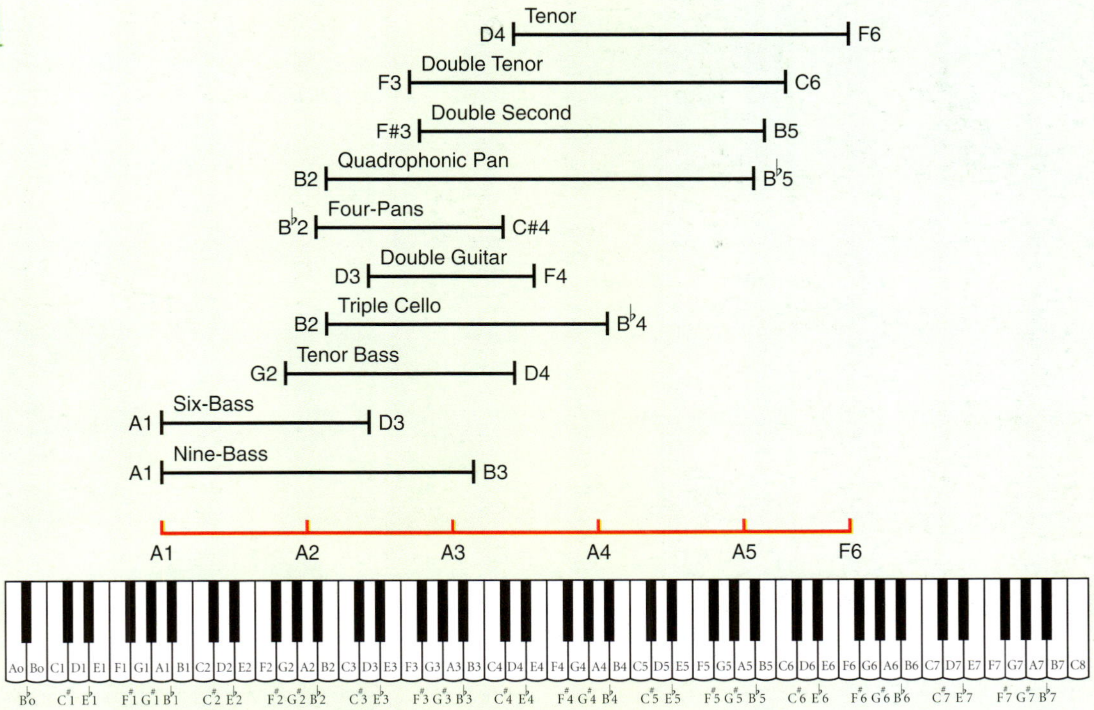

Chart showing the range of the various steelband instruments.

The *tenor kittle*, containing three slightly higher notes, was also slung diagonally (like a military kettle drum). On this, simple riffs were played over and over, thus making the overall rhythm a little richer.

Finally, there was the *ping pong*. Made from a small paint can, this was tuned with as few as four or as many as eight vague notes. It was held with one hand and struck with a mallet in the other hand.

Additionally, some bands had bugles – mostly those like Casablanca which were close to the orphanage, whose inmates had access to conventional instruments. These played military reveilles and injected a martial spirit into the rhythm.

Unidentified steelband, 1950. Note the automobile brake drum (iron) and tune boom in the centre. Photo by Junia Browne, courtesy of the ***Trinidad Guardian*** *and the National Archives of Trinidad and Tobago.*

Over the next half-decade there was a metamorphosis which created the modern steelband. The hand-held ping pong became the much larger tenor pan and the second pan. These lead instruments were slung around the neck and played with two sticks.

The biscuit drum boom first acquired notes to become the *tune boom*, before being supplanted by the large *bass*, made from an oil drum. Until wheels were added around 1959, the bass was restricted to stage settings, however, allowing the lighter tune boom to continue to be used on the road. Today, a single bass consists of between four and nine oil drums.

Between the front-line tenor and second pans, and the background basses, an array of mid-range instruments evolved out of the du dup and the tenor kittle, in order for all the notes on the chromatic scale to be covered. These included the *guitar* and *cello pans*, which were mainly used for 'strumming' chords.

Once the steelband acquired its full melodic capacity, the bugle was dropped. But the iron, still the loudest instrument in the ensemble, lives on.

Not that it has not changed. Brake hubs are now made of inferior metal, an aluminium alloy, so the iron has to be specifically fabricated from steel to retain the rich resonance with which it co-ordinates and paces all the other instruments.

More importantly, the iron is now tuned, and a band might have its iron section playing three different notes.

4-note ping pong

Ellie Mannette's 19-notes pan

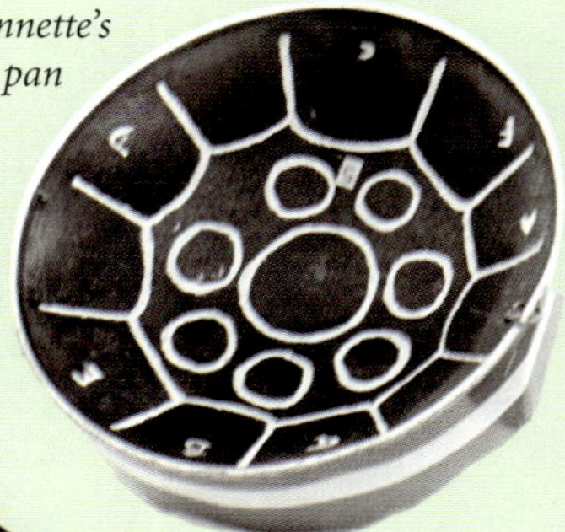

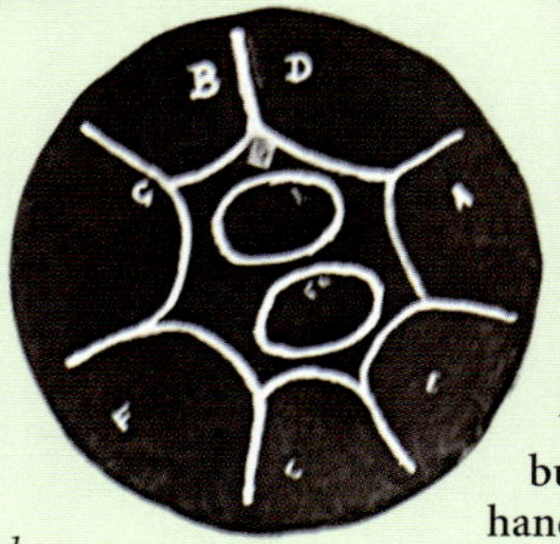

early second pan

Instruments property of PanTrinbago. Photo courtesy of the Information Division of the Office of the Prime Minister.

The evolution of the steelpan was propelled by the quest for notes. The du dup bass started with two, after which the ping pong took the lead. From four bumps on the bottom of a hand-held paint pan, Ellie Mannette sank the face into a convex bowl on an olive oil drum. He and other tuners steadily increased the number of its notes to eight, twelve, sixteen, and heightened their precision. In 1946 Sun Valley's Sonny Roach introduced a seven-note alto pan to play in harmony with the ping pong, and a next step in musical complexity was made. After someone from a small band in the country village of Tacarigua introduced the 55-gallon oil drum in late 1947, tuners pushed the number of notes on the lead pan up to nineteen, twenty-four, and higher. The larger face of an oil drum could fit more notes, and its thicker steel held them more accurately and durably. Its bowl was pounded deeper so that the stretched steel sang in a higher voice, until today's twenty-eight notes are tuned at concert pitch into the soprano range.

Not surprisingly, the ping pong evolved into the lead pan; and the alto pan became the second pan; those two being the main melodic voices of the bands. Less rationally, the ping pong acquired the name 'tenor pan', despite its notes being in the soprano range. The tenor kittle, whose notes were much lower, became the cello pan.

Scratcher and irons, Renegades, 1999.

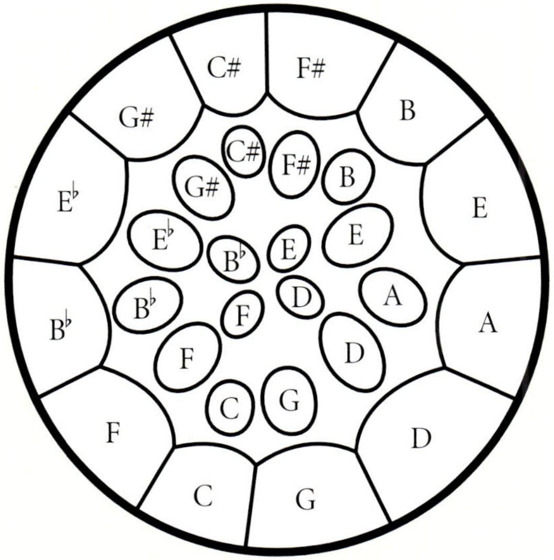

Diagram of a modern 28-note tenor pan.

A small section of Invaders in the early 1950s. The two flat pans in front are different-sized tenors. The two diagonal ones in the front are tune booms. The man in stripes in the back row plays a two-note du dup.

Invaders captain Ellie Mannette was the country's leading tuner. His tenors sounded the 'sweetest', and their design, with a large F# in the centre, was copied by many other tuners. Today Mannette, the 1999 recipient of the US Presidential Endowment for the Arts, is a professor of music at West Virginia University.

Considered the Stradivari of steel, Mannette is, however, only one of the many gifted innovators such as Anthony Williams from North Stars, Sonny Roach from Sun Valley, Neville Jules from All Stars, Croppy Simmonds from Casablanca, Alan Gervais from Tropical Harmony, Bertie Marshall from Hilanders, and others who invented and continue to elaborate this instrument.

And yet the first modern steelband was not the creation of any panman. Police bandmaster Lieutenant Joseph Nathaniel Griffith, as musical director of the 1951 Trinidad All Steel Percussion Orchestra (TASPO), had its members design pans to cover the entire chromatic scale from soprano to bass. TASPO combined eleven of the country's top pan players/tuners (including Mannette), to perform at the Festival of Britain in London.

Photo courtesy of Junia Brown.

TASPO introduced the cello pan and the bass, both of which were made from several oil drums. They gave the ensemble a melodic capacity in the middle and lower range for the first time. Griffith made every pan carry the chromatic sharps and flats within its range. He created musical arrangements that used full chords and harmonies. It was, to the steelband community, a revelation.

Ultimately, all pans are percussion instruments. You strike them to produce the sound, which makes them inherently rhythmic. But the steelband's continued link with its roots in the African drum calls for a more emphatic rhythmic base, if the music is to reach you in the gut. This is where the iron comes into its own.

For this job it has been supplemented by a host of other non-melodic instruments, rattles and scrapers and drums, which are grouped together to form the 'engine room' – the power in the band. Here you find the scratchers, the shak shaks, the African congas and timbales, the drum kit, the tambourines, and of course the iron, because, as calypsonian David Rudder sang, 'Something in the rhythm does tell them where they coming from'.

A family of instruments

The lower a note was on the scale, the bigger it was on the pan, and the thicker the steel needed. Tenor pans have a deep bowl which fits 28 to 30 notes. Fewer lower tones, however, can fit on a single drum. Tuners created new pans, by varying the depth of the bowl and the size of the notes; and they multiplied the number of drums, even in the higher range, giving you today's double tenors, whose 32 to 34 notes make them the choice of soloists; double seconds; double and triple guitars; triple and four-cellos; four-, six- and nine-basses.

Nine-drum bass.

Mid-range pans

One Christmas around 1950 Neville Jules, the captain, arranger and tuner of the Trinidad All Stars steelband, heard someone strumming a cuatro in a *parang* band and created a pan to provide the same rhythmic effect in his steelband. He called it the cuatro pan, although it became popularised as the guitar pan, an integral part of the mid-range section of every steelband.

Guitar pan.

No wonder the arranger who focuses most on the guitar pans should have begun music on a cuatro: Renegades' arranger, Jit Samaroo.

The earliest guitar pan was a single drum, and its invention was followed by that of the cello pan, which covered the range of notes immediately below. Both pans expanded to include multiple drums.

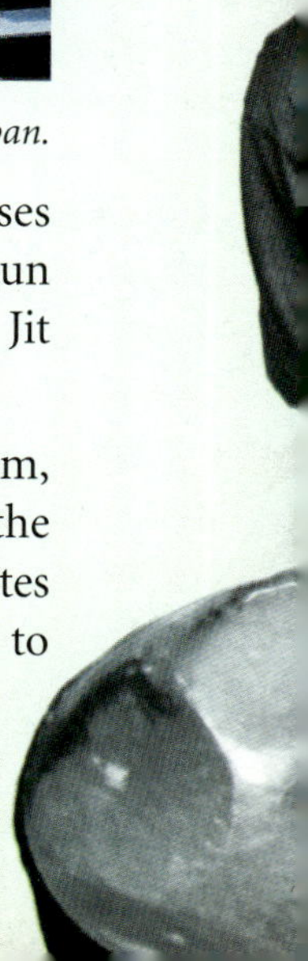

The sound of the guitar pan
Is something to talk about
Specially if the guitar man
Have the knowledge to bring it out.
He needs the ability
to give you the proper chords
The drive and the energy
And brother,
if he can prolong and get it right,
I guarantee the band would sound like dynamite.

('Guitar Pan' by Lord Kitchener)
Courtesy of Ice Music

Today guitar pans come with two or three drums. In the simplest arrangements they strum chords much as a reggae guitar does, providing one of the basic rhythms of the band. A more complex arrangement, however, such as those for which Jit Samaroo is famous, challenges the guitar pan players with their own intricate counter-melodies, spreading the three or four notes that comprise a chord among different players.

Extending the guitar pan's range both upwards and downwards are the 3- and 4-cellos, and more so the quadrophonics. Anthony Williams introduced the four-pan in the tenor range to play a passage in Von Suppé's 'Poets and Peasants Overture' in 1966; and Rudolph Charles created the quadrophonic in the late 1970s.

◀ *Renegades player Beverly Gomez-Brown on the three-cello.*

Renegades' stage side, Reunion Island, 1991. Photo courtesy of Michael Marcano.

Stage sides and Panorama bands

Steelband ensembles vary. There are stationary 'stage sides', which perform at concerts or dances. And there are Panorama bands. Renegades' stage side can be large – up to 40 players. Small bands may have six or seven. For all their variations, however, every stage side is fundamentally different from a 100-player Panorama band. Not only is the latter much larger; its pans are mounted on racks. The rhythm section is large and powerful. And in full swing a Panorama steelband literally jumps with energy.

Until 1961 pans were strung around the neck of the players, one pan to a man. But you can't play very much on the three notes of a single bass drum. So the first wheeled pans were the bass, and immediately afterwards the double seconds also went mobile. Players still walked behind their instrument, however: a difficult feat, depending on the rhythm of the music. From the sixties, racks were made which carried several pans, the players themselves and the canopies.

Quadrophonic pan, 1997.

This entrance to Harpe Place lasted till it was replaced by housing projects in the 1960s. Photo circa 1964.

La Cour Harpe

It was in such yards as La Cour Harpe that Afro-Trinidadians celebrated their freedom and fashioned their expressive culture with great verve and passion.

This culture was communal and public. It involved singing and dancing and drumming, which were held in any open space inside the yard where a bamboo tent and benches could be built. Some yards were famous for stickfighting. Others were better known for gambling and drinking. Most of them brought out Carnival masquerade bands. These were the seedbeds of the steelband movement.

A minute's stroll from Basilon Street, at the foot of the Laventille hills, there is a small triangle on the flatland, bounded by Oxford Street – on which Renegades has its pan theatre today – Observatory Street, and the East Dry River. Officially called Teschier Terrace, this spot is unofficially known as Harpe Place. Its original name, La Cour Harpe, harks back to a former owner of the land, and translates literally as The Harpe Courtyard. Before the war La Cour Harpe hardly lived up in appearance to its grand appellation, for it contained but a sprinkling of barrack apartments and old wooden shacks surrounding an open space and a tamarind tree that overhung the Dry River. There was a makeshift bench or two on which a homeless or drunk man might be seen dozing.

Yet simple as it was, in the tamboo bamboo era it had a reputation as one of the city's focal points of *jamette* life, that demimonde of calypsonians, street fighters and their followers. There, on pre-war Carnival Sunday nights, Dame Lorraine, a sort of variety show and burlesque with strong sexual overtones, was performed in a bamboo tent. For Carnival itself Lucien Gabriel, a descendant of a former owner of the Harpe, brought out a large Red Indian band from the yard. Gabriel also organised a calypso tent there in the 1930s, the Poet's House. La Cour Harpe was most famous, however, for being Port of Spain's main stickfighting venue. In its clearing was the ring – called a *gayelle* – in the centre of which was scooped out a 'blood hole' into which defeated combatants dripped the blood from their wounds. 'It had a bamboo tent – just seats, no roof', recalls Joseph Baird. 'As boys we'd sneak in and take a look. Sometimes, all of a sudden, I hear "Pow!" and my mother scramble me from behind.'

That was where practitioners of that martial sport, challengers from throughout the country as well as local champions – men with fearsome reputations such as Guta, Sampalai and Cut Outer – savaged one another with three-foot lengths of hardwood, all the while singing their boastful chants to the rhythms and chorus of a tamboo bamboo band:

When I dead bury my clothes
I don't want no sweetman to wear my clothes
When I dead bury my clothes
Not even my cousin must wear my clothes.

One of the few remaining wooden houses of La Cour Harpe with the outhouse and standpipe that provide sanitation and running water, 1997. Second picture in foreground: stickfighters, probably late 1950s. Photo courtesy of the ***Trinidad Guardian*** *and the National Archives of Trinidad and Tobago.*

At the far right, Andy Duncan, captain 1995–1999; next to right, Kelvin 'Pelican' Brown; at the left, Wallace 'Ako' Paul at the corner of Siparia Hill and Bath Street, where Bar 20 was based. At the top of Siparia Hill Felix 'Popwell' Barrio started Eighth Army, a band which lasted only a few months.

The Poet's House and the Dame Lorraine, the stickfighters and the tamboo bamboo were all swept away in the early 1940s by the growing steelband movement. Nevertheless, Harpe Place retained much of its tradition as a centre for *jamette* culture. There the Bar 20 men from nearby Bath Street idled and gambled, drank rum and consorted with their female counterparts, the prostitutes. When in 1943 the young Aldwyn Roberts arrived from the country town of Arima to make his name as the calypsonian Lord Kitchener, he found succour in the Harpe.

Kitchener rose to become arguably the greatest calypsonian ever. Certainly he is the greatest calypsonian to sing for and about the steelband movement: the only one who has had at least one of his tunes played by at least one steelband at every Panorama but one since the competition began. And his second steelband calypso, sung for the 1946 Carnival, was about Bar 20 on VE Day:

Zigilee, Pops and Battersby
They coming with a semitone melody
When they start this contrary beat
They had people jumping in the street
Port of Spain was catching afire
When the steelband was crossing the Dry River
Zigilee, leader of the ping pong
Had people jumping wild in the town

('The Beat of the Steelband')
Courtesy of Ice Music

'My mother never wanted me there – Basilon Street and La Cour Harpe to her was a place where they had these badjohns,' says Ricko Alexander, a Renegades pioneer.

Young men of Harpe Place still gather as they did a half-century ago in the shade of the tamarind tree that overlooks the Dry River.

Lord Kitchener

A century ago, when Carnival bands sang their call-and-response chants, the lead singer or chantwell alternated with the chorus. The two formed a unity to the accompaniment of tamboo bamboo percussion.

By the time Aldwyn Roberts was born in the country town of Arima in 1922, however, the chantwell had begun to distance himself from the band and was well on the way towards establishing himself as an independent entertainer – a calypsonian. The year before, 'Chieftain' Walter Douglas had formed the first commercial calypso revue. Grouped in what is called to this day a calypso 'tent', singers now performed for an audience seated on rented chairs under a tarpaulin. Moreover those first calypsonians, at least in the larger towns, had abandoned the rough accompaniment of tamboo bamboo percussion in favour of guitars, cuatros and clarinets, and in the thirties saxophones and trombones.

By adolescence Aldwyn Roberts' voice was already powerful and he served as a chantwell for a Carnival band and sometimes for gangs laying railway lines. He also sang calypso, winning the Arima Calypso King title from 1938 to 1941.

The next year, Roberts headed for the bright lights of Port of Spain where the wartime presence of thousands of US servicemen had put a premium on entertainers. He landed in La Cour Harpe and was befriended by prostitutes who put up to get him a suit in which to sing. There he also met the men and women from Bar 20.

Lord Kitchener. Photo 1940s.
Courtesy of the ***Trinidad Guardian.***

In 1944 the Arima champion was given the sobriquet Lord Kitchener, after his hit 'Green Fig' made him one of the most sought-after calypsonians. Around that time he sang his first steelband song, 'A Dream In My Cacheau'. On VE (Victory in Europe) Day, 8 May 1945, the wider public danced to steelbands for the first time. Kitchener took note and for the upcoming Carnival produced 'The Beat of the Steelband'. For calypso in general this was a sort of spiritual homecoming. The tamboo bamboo, which the chantwell had left so long before, had metamorphosed into the steelband, to which calypsonians now returned.

Kitchener left Trinidad for England in 1947. All the while he composed calypsoes which became hits back home. In 1963 he returned, and his tune 'My Pussin' won his first official Road March title.

1963 was also the first year of the Panorama competition. Thereafter, for every subsequent Panorama but one, a Kitchener calypso was played by some band in the finals. In the 1980s and 1990s Renegades played Kitchener's tunes fifteen times in the Panorama finals.

His remarkable achievement ended like the grandfather's clock on 11 February 2000, when the poet laureate of the steelband movement died. Kitchener had sung 'Pan Birthday', but for the first time in history no steelband played his tune in Panorama.

But boys will be boys, and some of the young Ohio Casanovas surreptitiously visited Harpe Place, where they made friends with the boys in another little steelband, East Side Kids.

That band was organised in 1945, after the demise of Bar 20, by 15-year-old Rudolph 'Rock' Carter, today a steelband stalwart in New York under the name Rudy King. Its leading members included Kim Loy Wong, who is now languishing in a Californian jail for drug-related offences, and Renegades pioneers Wallace 'Ako' Paul and Randolph Trotman, all of whom quickly became tuners.

The precise chronology is vague, but some time after the destruction and revival of the Ohio Casanovas, East Side Kids fell apart. Kim Loy Wong moved to another part of Laventille where he formed Hilanders, and Rudolph Carter migrated to the United States. Ako became involved with another band, Eighth Army, but that band got into a disastrous fight with the violent steelband Red Army and never recovered. Consequently, a handful of the former East Side Kids found their way into the Basilon Street band that was headquartered in the quarry.

As the only flat space available to Basilon Street youths, the quarry had long been their meeting place. As children they used to explore its cavernous fissures; grown older they held sporting competitions in its vast, stony amphitheatre from whose parapet the band's bugler, 'Mad Frankie', once threatened to parachute. They stored their pans in the abandoned kiln in the quarry. There the small, nameless band organised a fête to mark its formal launch on Empire Day, 24 May 1948.

The youths collected money, food and drinks from people in the neighbourhood: Royal Cup soft drink from the Xavier factory on Oxford Street, El Toro wine from somewhere else. That evening the band hit the road for the first time, tramping around a few quick blocks and dashing back into the quarry before the police could catch them.

Since the inception of the movement in 1939 steelbands had taken their names from movies, particularly war movies whose names were redolent of violence and against-all-odds heroism. Upper Laventille had the Desperadoes, John John had Destination Tokyo, Belmont had Rising Sun, Woodbrook had Invaders, nearby Oxford Street had Casablanca, and so on. Yet somehow, nothing caught the Basilon Street band's fancy. They tried out Bad Men of Missouri for size but it did not last; another year they opted for Dodge City. Unlike many other steelbands, the Basilon Street group was still fluid, still lacking a clear identity. Today there is no agreement even as to who was captain because this role at the time, like the names the band tried and discarded, meant so little. Then some time in the late 1940s an obscure movie was shown in the nearby Royal cinema: 'The Renegade', starring Larry Parks. Perhaps it fitted nicely with the band's skull-and-crossbones insignia, or maybe it accorded with their sense of being small and insignificant yet determined to prevail. For whatever reason, the youths were unanimous on the name of their band: the Renegades Steel Orchestra.

East Dry River

It raining, it raining, you hear the music in the mud
Sounding like a real symphony (...)
Coming down, oye, river coming down

(Lord Kitchener 'Mystery Band')
Courtesy of Ice Music

Amoco Renegades won the 1995 Panorama with this tune. In it Kitchener tells of a mystery band which plays in the Dry River whenever it rains, but which no one has ever seen. Crowds gather, the excitement grows and everyone offers his

The view from the Oxford Street bridge over the East Dry River separating Harpe Place (to the left) from Charford Court (to the right).

Young men in Harpe Place, 1997.

opinion, until the mystery is revealed. The river itself makes the music, knocking discarded bottles and the pans it bears in its streaming water.

This image of this elusive band evokes the early days of the steelband movement when the area around the Dry River teemed with bands and the river, usually a mere trickle (except when heavy rains flooded it), offered an escape route for illegally parading bands to dodge the law. Paved since 1934, the river was a playground for boys who raced home-made boats, played football or cricket, gambled, smoked cigarettes or just hung out. It was their space. In the era of steelband warfare it was divided into bitterly defended zones of influence.

To the east of La Cour Harpe it was easy to disappear into the maze of lanes, yards and drains that led to the top of Basilon Street and the quarry. On the other side was the river. A large space thus existed in which youths could melt away when they needed to.

West of the river lay Charlotte Street and the parallel arteries leading north to the Savannah and south to the downtown area. Charlotte Street was a main line between East and West Port of Spain. By the time Renegades came along, the section of Charlotte Street across from La Cour Harpe had seen better days. Its once elegant homes were now just rundown houses. But two cinemas, the Royal and the Pyramid, attracted the young population. And nearby, at the corner of Park Street, stood the Rosary school and church. A few blocks south was the city's market, which moved in the 1960s but left behind many ground provision vendors and an ambience of West Africa, which shades into a bustling cheapside of Chinese shops and clubs.

The 1960s also saw the rebuilding of La Cour Harpe. The old barrack houses, long sheds divided into rooms in which entire families lived, and the tumbledown shacks, were replaced by high-rise apartment projects. Two decades later similar buildings along Charlotte Street gave the two sides of the Dry River a resemblance.

Entrance to Charford Court on Charlotte Street. 1997.

Observatory Street, 1997.

Street-front shops and better-looking houses often hid barrack apartments whose dwellers frequently did odd jobs for the businesses or provided domestic help for the owners of the houses. A main thoroughfare from Belmont into the city, Observatory Street was partly commercial and, in the 1940s and 1950s, partly residential. During the 1960s better-off families retreated from the city to suburban areas, while working-class households moved to government housing, leaving behind the dark shops that remain today.

Drawing by Merille Manabir.

2

Badjohns

The Cracks, refuge of the young Renegades. Even today, after 50 years of urban overcrowding, this spot in what was once the Basilon Street quarry still evokes a sense of wildness and freedom, of maroonage in the heart of the slums: hence the local myth that runaway slaves hid there.

The Goldteeth years

Then as now, every steelband had its personality. Its size, its relations with the public and other bands, its approach to music, its very psyche were conditioned by the band's environment, and shaped by its experiences. But leaders, in the steelband movement as in politics, were strong personalities. In Renegades' case there emerged a powerful dynamic between the ambiance of the Basilon Street/La Cour Harpe districts in the 1950s and the band's captain, Stephen 'Goldteeth' Nicholson. He was a violent, autocratic man, a street-fighter who nevertheless had a winning charm, and this combination of repulsion and attraction pulled the band into the maelstrom of gang warfare, but also gave it the toughness to endure.

Those days steelbands blossomed everywhere like wildflowers in the rainy season. There were over a hundred steelbands in the country, according to one cautious estimate, with 59 in Port of Spain alone. Most were short-lived. Without at least one exceptionally gifted member, charismatic in his playing, arranging or tuning, a steelband found itself hard-pressed to survive. And if Renegades now had a name, an identity, still the band seemed stagnant. There were little competitions throughout the city in the Carnival season, but not one could they win, being overshadowed by their surrounding neighbours Casablanca, City Syncopaters, Trinidad All Stars and Hill 60. In 1950, when twelve of the country's best panmen were selected for the Trinidad All Steel Percussion Orchestra (TASPO) that would represent the colony at the Festival of Britain, Renegades was not even considered.

They had an excellent player and tuner in Yankee Boy, who could tune a dozen pans in a day. But it was a time when rebellious middle-class coloured and white kids were forming their own steelbands, and Yankee Boy preferred to hang out with them in West Port of Spain where his services were rewarded with hard cash.

As voluntary organisations, steelbands demanded considerable commitment. A continued lack of success could subject any one of them to strong centrifugal forces, which could only be contained by a fanatic loyalty and an iron discipline.

'Renegades was so small', quips Renegades pioneer Kirton 'Eddy Boom' Moore, about their fewer than fifteen members, 'the flagwoman coulda give the bassman a cigarette.' The flagwoman, Phyllis White, the mother of Renegade pioneer Cecil White, led the band, whereas the bassmen brought up the rear.

So one evening they asked Stephen Nicholson to take over the reins. The handsomest of Ma Belle James's five sons, he had come from Tobago as a child to live off Basilon Street in the early 1940s, and being an easygoing sort and an ardent sportsman he easily fell in with all the boys and teenagers in the district. Tall and athletic, he

Some Renegades pioneers. Goldteeth is shown in the middle (circa 1965), photo courtesy of Dude Baron. Top row, left to right: Cecil 'Dead' Hinkson; Kirton 'Eddy Boom' Moore; Ako and Martin 'Pancho' Benjamin. Bottom row, left to right: Ricko Alexander, Wallace 'Ako' Paul and Kelvin 'Pelican' Brown; at right Raymond 'Brokofoot' Pierre.

possessed noticeably long arms with enormous hands, and was an aggressive pace bowler for the Ohio Sports Club's cricket team. These physical and psychological qualities were also ideally suited to the other major activity for which he had a penchant – fighting.

Steelbands did not only play pan; they produced their own masquerades. At left here Desmond 'Bad Nigger' Baird, Joseph Baird's brother, plays a French sailor with Casablanca. 'Blanca and Renegades enjoyed a close fraternal relationship, and many men alternated between the two bands. Photo circa 1950, courtesy of Andy Duncan.

He knew everyone in the district, and everyone knew him, from the youngest to the oldest. He always had time for children and thought nothing of joining a group of little boys playing marbles. The older folk particularly liked him. He never tolerated any rambunctious behaviour or coarse language in their presence. To them Stephen was a gentleman, not a badjohn, for the Tobagonian in him showed great respect and courtesy to elders. To everyone outside the district, however, he was known and feared as 'Goldteeth'.

The steelband to which Goldteeth was first attached was Casablanca, around the corner at the top of Oxford Street. Musically, Casablanca was perhaps the hottest band in the country, and one of the most ambitious: by 1949 they were essaying Chopin's 'Nocturne in E Minor'. Maybe this is why Goldteeth first joined them, although he never played pan, just iron. The Casablanca men were more his age than were the younger Renegades. But it is also possible that he was drawn to the band's bellicosity, for the roughest Bar 20 characters had joined Casablanca once continuous police harassment destroyed their own band, and these men and the women they attracted had made Casablanca the most riotous steelband at the time.

In Renegades his first task was to secure their headquarters. Two members had stolen a canvas tarpaulin from a tyre shop down on Observatory Street, and used it to cover the band's tent in the quarry where Goldteeth sometimes lazed. The owner of the shop, a man named Samson, discovered where the tarpaulin had been taken, and being the strong, muscular man his name suggests, he marched up Basilon Street, chased off the young men in the quarry, shook down their tent and recovered his property. 'Samson', laughs Ako, 'shake down the temple.'

Goldteeth immediately took up the fire. He visited Samson and intimidated him so thoroughly he gave the tarpaulin to the youths.

Then Goldteeth turned his attention to the Renegades, organising new pans, imbuing a discipline in those teenagers with an iron fist. There was hardly a Renegade Goldteeth did not clobber at one time or another. Pelican Brown got it for taking some pans without permission, to play in a nightclub; Ako Paul for inadvertently not having his pansticks and strap on J'ouvert Morning – Ako stopped playing pan for Renegades as a result. So when Ricko Alexander decided he didn't feel like playing one year, Goldteeth put his foot down. He brought a new pan and gave it to Ricko with the words: 'You

Basilon Street falls away left to the quarry, Lubin Lane and Bath Street, where Renegades sought refuge at different times in the 1950s. Hidden by the bushes down behind the railing lived Stephen 'Goldteeth' Nicholson. Steelbands were scatttered throughout residential Port of Spain in those days; on Discovery Day, 31 August 1951, fifty-nine of them paraded its streets. Belgrade Street, running along the contour to the right, took you to City Syncopaters on Quarry Street. From there it was five minutes to Casablanca atop Oxford Street.

Those three, 'Blanca, Synco and Renegades, considered themselves to be related. So too did Joyland Synco when it was formed higher in Laventille. Many panmen shuttled between those bands. Even Ethelbert Serrette, who formed and destroyed the Ohio Casanovas, eventually resurfaced in Synco. Together they controlled the now-defunct Royal and Pyramid cinemas, located obliquely opposite one another on Charlotte Street.

Even further up the hill was Desperadoes, the king of the mountain; and down on the flat and south was Nelson Street's Sun Valley; both bands warred with Casablanca and Renegades at one time or another.

Trinidad All Stars also hovered nearby – on lower Charlotte Street in the 1950s – but made it a point of honour to keep away from the fighting as a band, whatever individuals may get up to. Just as the ***jamette*** *ambience of La Cour Harpe had shaped Bar 20, Casablanca and even Renegades, so too the sports-focussed self-discipline of Hell Yard, off Charlotte Street, had moulded the character of Trinidad All Stars.*

will play or you will walk [leave]'. 'I eh want nobody to rough me up and I eh leaving the band' recalls Ricko, 'so I learn the tune and play'.

Once, the younger men from the Harpe attempted, with a few of the Basilonians who gambled there, to hive off and form their own band, Meloharps. They bought Shell drums, had them tuned, and painted them yellow, blue and red: two tenors, a guitar pan and a second pan. Cecil 'Dead' Hinkson, though a Basilonian, was their captain.

'Two ships cyar leave from the same port the same time', declared Goldteeth. Meloharps fled, camping out in another neighbourhood. Meloharps stayed away for Christmas, and then the feud fizzled out and everyone was back in Renegades for Carnival.

Over those years, Goldteeth imprinted his forceful personality on the band. It kept them together through a long lean period – a feat which hundreds of bands didn't accomplish – but it also got Renegades

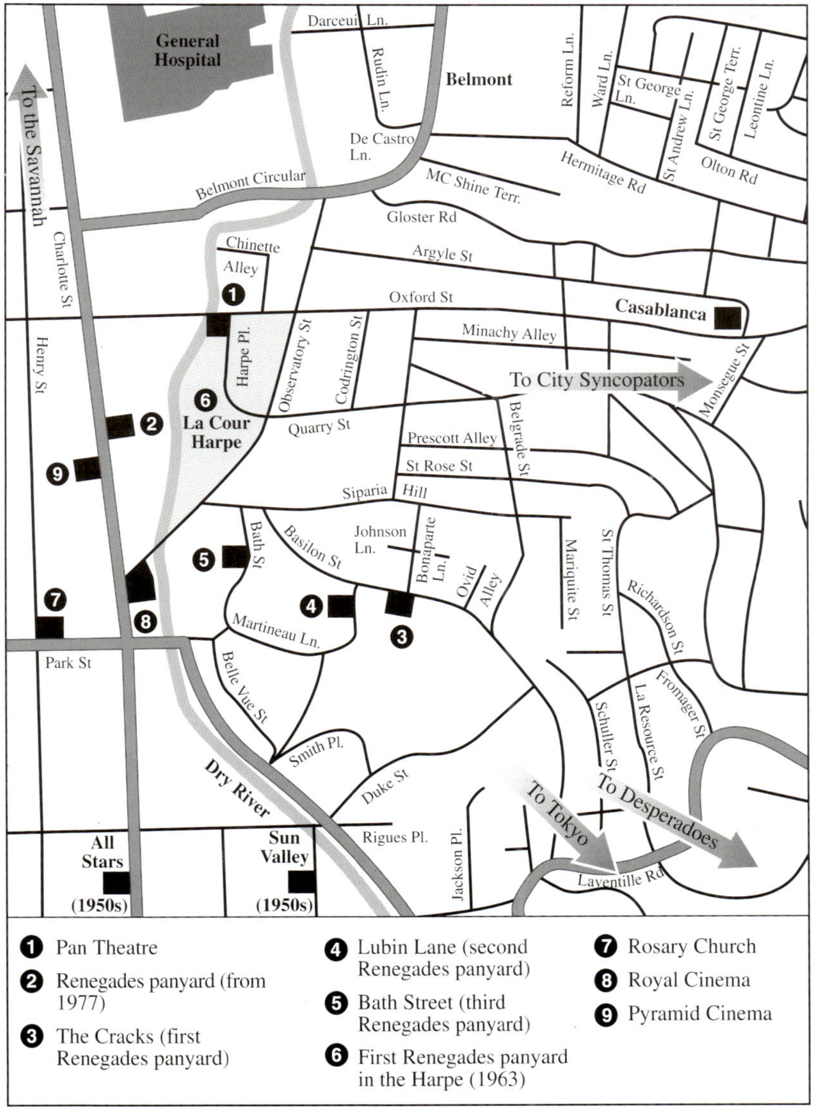

Renegades moved many times until they finally found a permanent home on Charlotte Street. The band's successive yards are numbered. Sites of other bands indicate their most frequent location during the 1950s and 1960s.

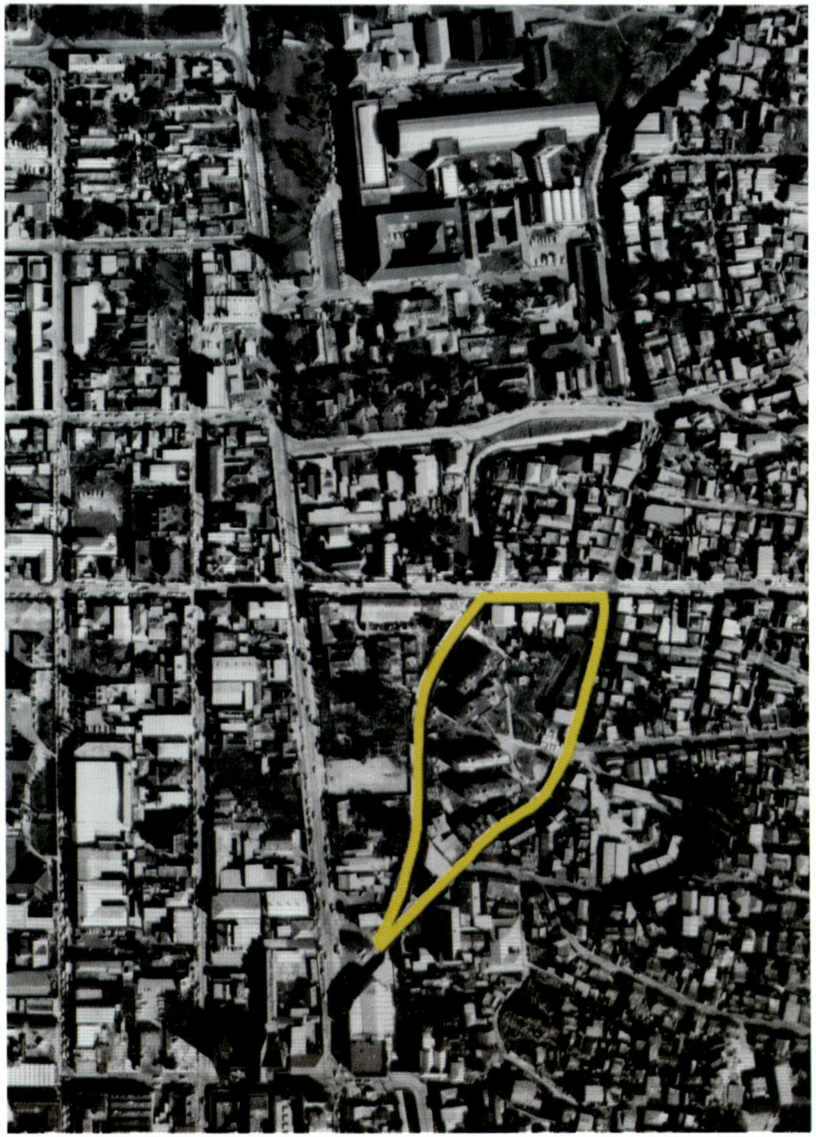

Aerial map, circa 1960, Courtesy of the Office of Land and Surveys. The yellow area marks the location of La Cour Harpe.

into fights with a dozen other steelbands, sometimes several at the same time.

The 1950s were the era of steelband warfare, of West Side Story feuds and affrays which erupted on the slightest of pretexts. Men from rival steelbands, whenever they met – on the streets at Carnival time, in dances or in the cinema – slashed one another with cutlasses or stabbed each other with ice picks. On the roads they hid cutlasses and bottles in bass pans, and when bands clashed, blood flowed.

Since 1948 Casablanca had been involved in a protracted and vicious feud with Invaders from Woodbrook, to the west of the city, which created deep enmities between those districts. Members and supporters beat, stoned and chopped one another whenever they met. The feud prompted the creation in 1949 of the Steelbands Association of Trinidad and Tobago – the forerunner to today's Pan Trinbago – in an effort to bring peace. It failed. And when Goldteeth became the captain of the Renegades, they too reaped the whirlwind.

'One Sunday we went to play cricket in the Savannah and Invaders come with baseball bat,' recalls Ricko Alexander. 'They say we is young Casablanca and they beat us. When we put Goldteeth as captain we put a problem.'

Fight for so between Invaders and Tokyo
Mama when these two bands clash
If you see cutlash
Never me again to jump in a steelband in
Port of Spain

Invaders beating sweet
Coming up Park Street
Tokyo coming down Frederick Street beating
slow
And when the two bands clash
Mama, if you see cutlash
Never me again...

(Mighty Blakie 'Steelband Clash')
Courtesy of Ice Music

***Trinidad Express**, 11 February 1959. After he sang 'Steelband Clash' in 1954, calypsonian Blakie went on to wave the flag for the belligerent San Juan All Stars in 1959 when they portrayed 'Battle Cry' and attempted to barge through Desperadoes, who were on Charlotte Street playing 'Noah's Ark'. Thus the most memorable clash in steelband history was sparked. Tokyo came up behind San Juan All Stars and joined the fray. Appropriately the battle took place in front of the Colonial Hospital: dozens of panmen ended up in the casualty department, and more passed through in flight. In the panic that ensued, the spectacular pieces created by Cito Velasquez for the band ('Flowers and Fruit') were almost entirely destroyed. By then the violence had begun to wane, however, its most serious manifestation having occurred six years before, when the 1953 celebration for the coronation of Queen Elizabeth II saw scores injured and a passer-by beaten to death with baseball bats.*

War!

Like the stickfighters of the past, steelbands were combative organisations. Renegades were too small to take part in the battle between major bands during Carnival. But they carried on long-lasting feuds with enemies that earned them a ferocious reputation.

30 Injured In Steelband Clash

Battleground By Hospital

5 Hurt In Sangre Grande

Desperadoes, Carnival 1951, portraying the film 'To Hell and Back'. Courtesy of the Information Division of the Office of the Prime Minister.

From the late forties, violence and steelband were considered synonymous. Not in the smaller towns and villages but in Port of Spain, whenever large bands met on the streets, there was a good chance an all-out battle would ensue. This occurred frequently at Carnival time for there were many bands and no prescribed routes. Two bands could be travelling in opposite directions, or a faster-moving band could catch up with one in front. Often nothing untoward happened. The bands passed, friends waved at one another or stopped for a chat and a drink. Sometimes, in a spirit of benign rivalry, the bands might hold an impromptu competition, each one playing its best tune. Thus was born the Bomb competition.

Such an encounter, however, could turn nasty. It could become a clash.

One band might be louder than the other whose players went off rhythm. An aggressive flag-waver might hit someone as he swished and twirled the flag. A mischief-maker only had to throw an orange into one band: bottles and stones flew, crowds scampered for cover, pans dropped, baseball bats, cutlasses and razors emerged from their hiding places and men attacked.

Almost every band had its fair share of fighters; men who enjoyed a good tussle or who just never backed down. And some larger steelbands, notably Casablanca, Tokyo, Red Army and Invaders, made it a speciality, approaching other bands with a belligerent air.

Apart from those spectacular clashes there were the more destructive feuds between bands, wars of attrition that could drag on for years in which posses would make raids into the enemy's territory to attack anyone associated with the other band. Entire districts in the city were out of bounds for some panmen.

Such feuds – called 'riots' in Trinidad – could be sparked by any fight between members of two bands. Women who were friendly with members of rival bands often started riots of sporadic violence throughout the year.

The aggressive territoriality of the steelbands was a long tradition. Indeed, steelbands were more cohesive than the traditional Carnival bands. Instead of loosely structured seasonal groups, they were tightly knit, perennial organisations. The rivalry was amplified – in size, volume, masquerade, instrumentation, music, women, in everything. And the postwar recession intensified tensions, especially in the cities where conditions were harsher and traditional constraints weaker.

The explosion of steelband violence and in particular the feud between Invaders and Casablanca prompted the formation of the Steel Bands Association. Similarly it was the feud between Desperadoes and Tokyo in 1958 that nudged the government towards setting up a Special Works programme for the unemployed youth. The fighting declined in the 1960s, and by the end of the decade it was a thing of the past. The initiatives it inspired, however, the unemployment relief and the corporate sponsorship of steelbands, continue to the present.

Goldteeth wasn't alone, of course. Beside him were men like Desmond 'Bad Nigger' Baird, another fist fighter, and Sonny 'Zwill' Trust, who was handier with a knife. ('Zwill' refers to the pieces of razors stuck on kite tails for cutting the thread on other kites.) When the band tramped around Port of Spain at Carnival, Goldteeth and the other fighters prowled in front wearing army jackets and glaring ferociously at larger passing steelbands, while the younger Renegades quaked.

'People didn't like us, they didn't know it was the older ones who get us involved', says Ricko. 'I had to be in it but I didn't like it.'

Ironically, just when middle-class youth were joining the steelband movement this internecine warfare intensified to instil fear and loathing in respectable people of all classes. Thus Renegades' growing notoriety, like that of many another band, kept away masqueraders, pan players, and even people from its own community. Fathers would beat a daughter caught speaking to a panman; mothers forbade their sons to join a steelband. Some of the Renegades players had to avoid the band until it was far from home before they could take a chance to play.

Not that the band did not rehearse regularly: Goldteeth made sure of that. They even divided into two sections and practised passing one another so that when the band met another on the street its different

Portrait of a warrior

The following extract from Earl Lovelace's The Dragon Can't Dance gives us a glimpse of what the author calls 'the warriorhood' of the steelbandsmen. In a novel that has become a classic fictional representation of Carnival, Lovelace presents the ordinary people at the heart of that festival and of the steelband movement. Fisheye is such a character, a badjohn who becomes a warrior in the service of the emerging pan culture.

For all the years he remained in Calvary Hill steelband, he never became a real steelbandsman, a musician. ... From the first, he was a warrior, a fighter, entering bodily into the violence boiling in the guts of the city; and soon everyone on Calvary Hill would know his name – for those were the days when every district around Port of Spain was its own island, and the steelband within its boundaries was its army providing warriors to uphold its sovereignty. Those were the war days, when every street corner was a garrison; and to be safe, if you came from Belmont, you didn't let night catch you in St James; if your home was Gonzales you didn't go up Laventille; and if you lived in Morvant you passed San Juan straight.

In this war, in this army, Fisheye at last found the place where he could be a man, where his strength and quickness had meaning and he could feel pride in belonging and purpose to his living, and where he had all the battles he had dreamed of, and more, to fight. While he was with them, Calvary Hill became a name to be respected, to be spoken of with the same measure of awe with which young men whispered Desperadoes, Rising Sun, Renegades, Red Army, Hell Yard, Tokyo – bands that announced and advertised in their very names the fact and dreams of a violence they cultivated all year round, in constant battles fought between themselves, with razors, knives, in hand to hand combat, in night clubs, gambling houses and on street corners .... Calvary Hill became one of the tall names, joining with others to turn Carnival days to the celebration of their warriorhood, plunging into Port of Spain, costumed in warriors' robes, celebrating and invoking and lifting to god-hood, Ghengis Khan and Attila and Spartacus, Alexander, Hitler, Conquistadors, bandits, US Marines, making the city their arena, the savannah, their stage, parading, bragging their might, warming, stretching their limbs in the tough, hot, rejoicing steelband music their accompanying bands, after months of practising, had captured to exalt them .... Fisheye delighted in this living; and soon, his name had been added to the roster of heroes that ruled Port of Spain: Batman, Big Sax, Mastifay, Tom Keen, Zigilee, Baron and Barker.

Renegades, Carnival 1959, portraying the film 'Between Heaven and Hell'. The tradition of military and naval masquerades long predated the steelband movement. An Artillery band is already documented the year of Emancipation (1834). The martial theme and military model of organisation appealed to Afro-Trinidadians for they echoed the aristocratic and warlike traditions of their African past. Military units with their many ranks and uniforms recalled the elaborate hierarchies found in West African royal courts and secret societies, and provided images of heroism, pageantry, fantasy and caricature. From the 1920s on bands inspired from the British and later the American Navy became increasingly popular. Steelbands frequently played sailors or other forms of military mas, drawing freely on the rich stock of Hollywood war movies.

The fight between Renegades and Invaders

In the Invaders–Renegades feud, something similar to the old tradition of the stickfight was invoked when a duel was organised in the quarry one lunchtime between Goldteeth and Stanley 'Ponehead' Hunte – the man who honed Invaders into one of the most formidable fighting bands ever.

As a crowd of men from both bands watched, the two warriors circled one another and then clashed. The Invaders man was in the evening of his days while Goldteeth was younger and stronger and sought to rely on that, but Ponehead was more experienced. Quickly he tripped up Goldteeth and began to pummel him on the ground. They were separated and faced one another again. And again Ponehead got the better of Goldteeth. Another two gladiators were brought out: Leonard 'Slim' Joseph for Invaders and Harold 'Fowl' Lewis for Renegades. Fowl was a weightlifter, big and muscular, but his feet turned cold. The Renegades were being humiliated, so Baird stepped forward and challenged another Invaders man, Nathaniel 'Monster' Martin. Monster, however, was no more willing to fight than Fowl had been, and the whole tournament fizzled out. But it worked, because soon the feud between the two bands also fizzled out.

Thereafter, Invaders became one of the most important supporters of the struggling Basilon Street band. Invaders men arranged their 1962 Festival tune and tuned their pans. Their first important arranger, Trevor 'Brutus' Charles, was from Invaders, and indeed many Renegades players frequented the Woodbrook band's panyard to learn from them. In the sixties, when Renegades did not have enough pans to enter competitions they would borrow from Invaders, so that to this day Renegades is one of the two steelbands – the other being Desperadoes – still using the old Invaders style of tenor pan.

The Arouca Renegades

Arouca had no Carnival celebrations and some youths from the town used to play mas in Port of Spain with the Woodbrook middle-class band Nightingales until the latter collapsed after a fight with another band. Someone suggested the Aroucans try Renegades, and Bese, a leading member of the group, went to meet Goldteeth. 'I was surprised he knew so many of the Arouca guys', says Bese. 'I didn't know about Renegades' reputation but the friendship, the way they made country boys feel comfortable, made you stay. And then you know nobody eh go bother you.' The Aroucans were not afraid of a riot either. And as if to prove the point, they came out with the band for Coronation in 1953, bringing the baseball bats they had bought from the American base in Wallerfield.

Bese's group became known as the Arouca Renegades, the country boys making up half the band's players and masqueraders until the late fifties, by which time Goldteeth had brought in more outsiders from even further afield. 'I met Goldteeth in a fête in Palms Club in San Fernando and he asked us to play with them – he liked fellas from the countryside to play with them and he treated us good', says Cecil 'Punch' Cumberbatch. Punch was from Tunapuna but in the mid-fifties he worked in Fyzabad where he organised a group to spend a few days in Port of Spain by Goldteeth and play mas with the band: 'You come from the country and you get good treatment, you stick around. It only have one band in Trinidad for us, Renegades, and when they have any problem with fighting we gone down.'

rhythm would not confuse them. Indeed, Renegades was one of the handful of bands with a 'stage side': a small, permanent group of players who performed throughout the year in shows or parties. Renegades' stage side enjoyed a weekly gig at the Miramar, a nightclub in which Goldteeth worked as a bouncer. Such joints were common in the city, one stretch known as the Gaza Strip having half a dozen next to one another – a legacy of the Americans' presence during the war.

But Renegades contained no outstanding talent, so they never became a major musical force. The band would have suffered for recruits, and its growth would have been stunted, had Goldteeth not filled the breach by pulling in friends he had made on his frequent out-of-town jaunts. Again, it was his peculiar democratic gregariousness and perhaps his own rural roots that attracted the rustics who would have otherwise felt uncomfortable in town. Throughout the 1950s and early 1960s, the country boys made up half Renegades' players and masqueraders. The majority hailed from Arouca, a small village about eight miles from Port of Spain, but some came from as far as Fyzabad, in the south, and Toco and Matelot on the north coast.

Since TASPO the instrument had come of age, having attained what is essentially its modern form. Steelbands were playing full arrangements of many kinds of music, not only calypso. TASPO's repertoire included waltzes, rumbas, sambas, mambos, light classics, pop songs and calypsoes. From 1952 on, the biennial Music Festival, organised by the Trinidad and Tobago Music Society, had a component in which steelbands experimented with European classical music. In this scenario most top bands had the assistance of formally trained musicians, usually sympathisers from their neighbourhoods, and here again Renegades' pariah status limited its prospects.

Renegades, circa 1956, portraying the film 'Vera Cruz'. Photo courtesy of Andy Duncan.

So if they survived the 1950s, it was only just. In those days of gang warfare every steelband needed a police permit to play on the roads for Carnival or any public holidays, and it was withheld from troublemakers. Red Army was banned in the 1940s and changed its name to Lucky Jordan. Tokyo was banned too, and the members all played with Casanovas, a nearby kids' band. Renegades was banned one Discovery Day in the mid-1950s, and for the Carnivals of 1960 and 1961 they were refused permits to come on the road.

It was not surprising, because when Renegades went on the warpath no holds were barred. In a war against Sun Valley from Nelson Street, for instance, men were so badly damaged, one having his arm chopped off, that the court handed down stiff sentences on two Renegades: ten years and twelve strokes of the cat-o'-nine-tails each for Carl 'Tampico' Greenidge and Utah Blane.

On those two Carnivals when the band was prohibited from playing, Goldteeth and many Renegades joined City Syncopators. A few went to Trinidad All Stars, and the youths from the Harpe allied themselves to Casablanca. Those were significant choices, given that Casablanca fought with everyone, whereas All Stars never rioted, and Syncopaters was a peaceful offshoot from Casablanca. It was as if Goldteeth was trying to pull them in a different direction, to channel their energy into music. Once Renegades was allowed on the road again in 1963, he brought in Belgrave and Carlton 'Block' Bonaparte, two top panmen from the band Southern Symphony. Again they were out-of-towners, from Point Fortin in the far south, who happened to play in the Miramar nightclub. Alas, if Goldteeth hoped that the band would easily shake off the reputation that he had done so much to give it, he was badly mistaken.

*The Pyramid movie theatre on Charlotte Street. 1997. Trinidadians have always loved movies. Even the bookish V.S. Naipaul admits: 'nearly all my imaginative life during the long cramming years had been in the cinema' ('Reading and Writing', **New York Review of Books**, 2000, p. 22). Most steelbands were named after movies and they inspired many Carnival masquerades. Today steelband mas is a thing of the past, as are the movie theatres then frequented by Renegades. They were both torn down: the Royal in 1980 and the Pyramid in 2000.*

A song by Lord Laro

I've seen New York's greatest actors
Hollywood designers and Broadway producers.
But designers, actors and producers in
Carnival …
Broadway can't have nothing on them at all.

When you hear the tempo
The land vibrate with tempo
The island like one big disco,
Jamming soca, jamming, jamming calypso.
Hear them bassline grooving,
See them waistline moving,
Costumes of worth, rhythms like dirt,
It's the greatest show on the Earth.

(Lord Laro 'The Greatest Show on Earth')
Courtesy of KK Records

Photos and articles: from top to bottom; ***Trinidad Guardian****, 4 June 1965;* ***Evening News****, 13 January 1965;* ***Trinidad Guardian****, 14 January 1965. Courtesy of the National Archives.*

Lawbreakers

Teenage street gangs proliferated in the late 1950s in Port of Spain, much as in New York. Only, here they were usually affiliated to larger steelbands. Their casual nihilism was frowned upon by the older panmen, even those who were themselves no angels. But unlike many other bands, Renegades never disowned their Young Turks. Instead, these wild young men from La Cour Harpe were allowed, on the departure of Goldteeth, to assume leadership positions, so that the name they called themselves, the Lawbreakers, became synonymous in the 1960s with the band that nurtured and occasionally fought alongside them.

The tide was slowly turning. It was the era of independence, when the steelband movement was being promoted as the pride of the fledgeling nation's culture. The most belligerent bands were straining to end the internecine fighting, and channel their passions from martial combativity into musical competitiveness. With the Lawbreakers at the helm, however, Renegades swam against the current.

The older Renegades were discouraged. Although they had played in a few gigs, those two years off the road had broken their spirit. Under Goldteeth's supervision, 'Brokofoot' Raymond strove to pull them together, but there was a chance the band wouldn't re-group for the 1963 Carnival. 'So the younger fellas decide to take it over', recalls Rupert 'Small Axe' Mader. 'Me, Whitey, Tan Tan, Boldface, Mr Lee and some others went to Miramar and tell Goldteeth we want to bring out the band.'

Goldteeth replied: 'Take all the pans and carry it in the Harpe.'

It was an unpopular decision but he had realised that the older Basilon Street pioneers were becoming less active, that the band's warriors would soon be those younger men who limed in the Harpe and called themselves the Lawbreakers.

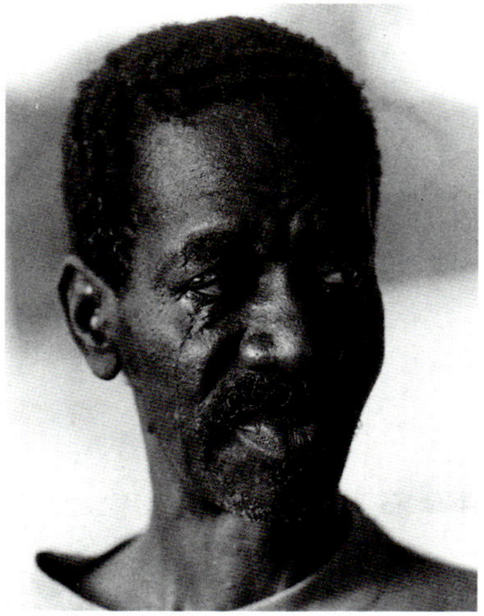

Roland 'Wawa' King, one of the Lawbreakers warriors (d.1999). 1997.

This was a gang similar to many others being formed in the slums and often loosely associated with their neighbourhood steelbands. Up in Laventille Thunderbirds attached themselves to Desperadoes. Around Nelson Street's Sun Valley sprouted Applejackers. In the west, Invaders acquired the Navarones. These young men observed no rules, and were often despised by the older steelband badjohns for their uncouth style, their penchant for petty crime and indiscriminate hooliganism.

'We was young', says Boldface Patrick, 'and the older fellas thought we was miserable.'

Although they were a sub-group of younger members in the band, not every Lawbreaker was a born and bred Renegade. Winston 'Dr Rat' Bruce and Trevor 'Bambi' Lowhar were; but Musso, Small Axe and his brother Albert 'Papito' Mader originally frequented Casablanca. From further afield came Horace 'Tan Tan' Johnson, Knolly and Ivan Shine, Lennard 'Boldface' Patrick and Oswald McSween, who used to be in Joyland Synco further up Laventille.

Joyland Synco was a splinter group from City Syncopators, which was in turn a breakaway from Casablanca, so there was a connection. Renegades, Casablanca and City Syncopators had always considered

Lennard 'Boldface' Patrick, Renegades captain (1971–1974, 1991–1994), beating iron. Photo courtesy of Andy Duncan. The iron is one of the instruments sometimes played by steelbands' captains and arrangers, even those who are virtuosos on other instruments, because it dominates the rhythm of the band but does not require time-consuming rehearsals.

We want work

About 120 placard-bearing, unemployed members of the Renegades steelband 'demanding work…or else' left their headquarters at Harpe Place, East Dry River, yesterday morning, and marched through busy streets of Port of Spain before settling at Woodford Square.

At the square, the youths, led by John Griffith, and under the watchful eyes of armed policemen from headquarters, shouted:

'We want work. We have a right to live. We want food. We want employment.'

Then there was quiet and a member said:

'The law says don't steal. But there is another law which says when you are hungry you must eat.'

Dole system

Another member of the group said that they were not against the police.

'We want the police to help us.'

Reverend Mr Jackson, of the Church of God, San Juan, took the mike and added his quota: 'I come to align myself with you and your problems because I am a Christian. If we don't help you, you will certainly not help us.'

Mr George Jeremiah was the best speaker. He said that there was a dole system in England whereby unemployed people were given something at the end of every week. Then he asked: 'What is happening to us in Trinidad and Tobago? Why can't we get the dole too?'

7 June 1964

Renegades demonstrators demand work.
***Trinidad Guardian**, 7 June 1964. Courtesy of the **Trinidad Guardian** and the National Archives.*

themselves to be closely related. Members of Joyland Synco used to walk down Basilon Street to go to the Royal Cinema, and when that band collapsed in 1961, some members migrated higher up the Hill to Desperadoes, but others such as McSween took their allegiance lower down into Renegades. Just then a scuffle took place at the Royal Cinema between a few Desperadoes and Lawbreakers. The older fighters joined the feud and the lines were drawn.

'One night I on the block on Laventille Road and a Despers squad come and accuse me of liming with Lawbreakers, and attack me. I get out and then I move down into the Harpe', says McSween. 'I start to play pan in Renegades in 1962 and I get six dollars. It was pleasing too because I play with all my heart.'

Despite the grumbling of the band's elders, Goldteeth took the captaincy away from Brokofoot Raymond in 1963 and gave it to McSween. Also in that year, and even more disconcertingly, Goldteeth, the lover of so many local beauties, married Judith Ann Weller, a white American anthropologist who had been working on a dissertation on East Indians in Trinidad. Immediately there were problems: to enter the US Goldteeth required special permission because of his record of convictions. As for Weller, the Trinidad authorities suspected her intentions: either she was mad or a Communist. Eventually, however, they got the necessary clearance and left Trinidad late in 1963, never to return. Towards the end of 1964 Stephen 'Goldteeth' Nicholson, a legend in his time, died of cancer in New York.

The times were changing. Trinidad and Tobago had become independent on the stroke of midnight, 31 August 1962, under the leadership of Black Nationalist intellectual Dr Eric Williams and his People's National Movement (PNM). Panmen, including the Renegades, worshipped 'The Doc', as Williams was called, for his vision of black redemption. Reciprocally, he saw the steelband movement as both the seedbed of national culture and a link with urban grass roots communities. In 1963 the government's Carnival Development Commission sponsored the first ever Panorama competition.

Although Williams was not above using panmen as his political thugs, he was also concerned over their gang warfare. Shortly after winning his first election in 1956 as head of the government that was to manage the transition to independence, Williams had instituted a make-work programme in Laventille, John John and San Juan, to be administered by Desperadoes, Tokyo and San Juan All Stars. In 1957 the Community Development Ministry had encouraged Goldteeth and George Beckles, a popular figure in the area and a supporter of the band, to form a youth group. In 1961 the same organisation (now the Community

Around the Harpe: Observatory Street and adjacent areas. At right Lambert 'Pinkeye' Lezama (d. 1999), one of the Lawbreakers. 1997.

Ossie Mc Sween, former Renegades captain (1962–1963), at the exit of an underground drain from Bath Street into the Dry River. 1997.

'The tunnel was a kinda escape route. If you battle with police, you jump in the Dry River and take that canal and come out in Bath Street. Or we used to take oil drums from the gas station by Royal Theatre, throw them in the Dry River and roll them up to the same tunnel. It was a short cut. Once you go in you come out in Bath Street. Matter of fact, if we liming by the theatre on the bridge, we'd jump down from the wall into the Dry River and most times we'd run up that tunnel if we not going in the Harpe.'

In Bath Street lived Muriel White. Having been a surrogate mother to the Bar 20 men of the early 40s, she now gave succour to the young Lawbreakers. The pans stolen at the gas station were carried through her yard up to Basilon Street.

Development Office) tried to negotiate a peace between the warring Lawbreakers and Sun Valley. 'The Lawbreakers said openly and emphatically that they would not stop rioting until they got work', recounts British social activist Darcus Howe, a former Lawbreaker. 'They went to the Community Development

Some of them eh lose their mama features yet
But they playing badjohn looking for death.
Sleep all day and night
Miserable always picking up fight
Their parents try but they fail
I know everyone of them dogs in jail.
...
I never see so much delinquency.
Everywhere they go theatre – twelve-thirty,
And believe me, they going in free.
One will call the gateman here,
Talk in he ears ten gone through there.
The gentleman rush to put up a stop
They push he down and he whole theatre full up.

Chorus:

They don't give a damn and they so far underage,
They just like a blasted orphanage.
The police should really interfere,
They too young for this criminal career.
Wash them clothes, give them food
And teach them not to be rude.
Don't let me catch them after six
Because any time ah see them is licks.

(The Mighty Sparrow 'Renegades')

Courtesy of Ice Music

Office and demanded that a Community Centre be sited in their area, which they would build themselves and for which they would be paid by Government. They also demanded a drum set.'*

McSween hadn't lasted as captain. Shortly after his appointment he was charged along with two other men for possessing firearms – previously unknown in steelband wars. Then in 1964 there was a fight amongst the Lawbreakers over a young woman, Brenda 'Chunks' Parson. Tan Tan was shot in the mouth. McSween and Rudolph 'Turkey' Thomas hid in the countryside but they were soon caught. Turkey got a dozen years, and although McSween won his case he was once again an ordinary tenor player in the band. Julian 'Jubal' Alexander, a senior and more stable Renegade from the Harpe, was

With Bar 20 matriarch Muriel White is the born and bred Renegades member Winston 'Dr Rat' Bruce, who does not play any instrument but helps the band with odd jobs such as painting the racks. Once a notorious Lawbreaker, he has been involved in several shootouts, and still enjoys some standing in underworld circles. In the 1970s and 1980s he spent much time in London with the Mangrove Steel Orchestra as a guest of another former Lawbreaker, ***Race Today*** *editor Darcus Howe. Photo 1997.*

Lawbreaker Rupert 'Small Axe' Mader and his brother Papito joined in 1962. Their sister Beryl also frequented the band . 'Small Axe' played tenor and tenor bass until the mid-1970s and now belongs to Renegades' senior members association. Like Dr Rat and other former Renegades he still lives in the Harpe where he grew up. He works, and has worked for most of his life, at construction sites. Photo 1997.

now captain. Still the Lawbreakers escalated the violence associated with the band to a higher plane.

Their turbulence continued the isolation of Renegades even from people of the neighbourhood, let alone outsiders. Indeed, it was their lack of the solid rump of community support that warring bands such as Desperadoes and Tokyo enjoyed, which prompted the Lawbreakers to even the odds by introducing guns into the equation. This increased their solitude.

As before, they recruited outlaws from the hinterland, this time a group from El Dorado, where McSween had hidden from the law in early 1964. These new auxiliaries, mainly East Indians, comprised an insignificant band named Rhythm and Blues. For the 1964 Carnival they joined Renegades in bringing out the mas 'Mongolian Hordes'.

From the viewpoint of the senior Renegades, however, that same

'The Unemployed and the Special Works', by Darcus Howe and Bukka Rennie, in Susan Craig (ed.) **Contemporary Caribbean: A Sociological Reader**, *Vol 2, 1982, pp.127–136.*

Renegades at the corner of La Cour Harpe and Observatory Street. The basses here are mounted on racks without canopies but some of the players carry their tenors manually, which together indicate that this took place in the early 1960s. Photo courtesy of Andy Duncan.

year was more significant for the launch of the East Port of Spain Youth Movement, whose first meeting was held in Martineau Lane, off Basilon Street. Its executive members were mostly senior Renegades. Newton 'Mouths' James was an officer, Jubal Alexander, the captain, was a trustee, and George Beckles president, and they worked to curb the gang fights flaring up in the city.

Beckles was important, though a strange figure in the equation. From up Calvary Hill, he was considered to be 'social' – that is, respectable. A clerk on the docks, he was also a boxing promoter. He never played pan but for some reason he made himself a sort of patron of the band. Perhaps the pugilist in him was sympathetic to them. He sometimes gave the prominent Renegades money, or maybe a bottle of scotch. He would invite them over for Christmas lunch. Generally, he advised them, and eventually became the band's public relations officer. Most importantly, he always sought an end to the violence.

Beckles was a member of the ruling PNM. He never made of Renegades a sort of plebeian arm of the party, as were Desperadoes and Tokyo. Instead he encouraged Renegades to agitate for a community centre in Basilon Street and for jobs. 'The committee strove hard to bring the warfare to a halt', wrote Beckles in his 'Report on East Port of Spain Youth Movement' written for the opening of the Youth Centre in November 1966. 'The government then instituted a crash programme and members of rival gangs found themselves working on the same projects at Laventille and around the Basilon Street and Harpe Place areas. This, more than anything else, promoted the welfare of the Youth Movement.'

The sixties were steelband's golden years. With state encouragement, companies sponsored bands to purchase better pans and hire better arrangers. By 1965 Desperadoes were sponsored by Coca Cola, Starlift by Angostura, Sundowners by Texaco, Cavaliers by Guinness, Savoys by Chase Manhattan, Tokyo by Carib, Harmonites by Solo, and North Stars by Pan Am. Their music acquired a mellow sweetness that was poised between yesterday's raw primitiveness and tomorrow's difficult complexity. The invention of wheeled pan racks allowed double pans and the heavy basses (formerly only used by stage sides) to now play on the roads. There the steelbands attracted by far the largest crowds of masqueraders on Carnival days.

Offseason they played the classics in the Steelband Music Festival, which, from its beginning as part of the Trinidad Music Festival in 1952, had become an

***Trinidad Guardian**, 1963. Courtesy of the **Trinidad Guardian** and the National Archives.*

independent competition. * The competition retained the format it already had in the Music Festival, in which each band performed a test piece, a calypso and a piece of choice, and the chosen tune from the start was almost invariably an excerpt from European classical music. That ascending scale was peaked in 1969 by the greatest band at the time, North Stars, when that band held its famous 'Ivory and Steel' public concert with the world-renowned concert pianist from Trinidad, Winifred Atwell. By then even the most disdainful critics were won over by the steelband movement, which had largely shunted the rivalry away from violent confrontation.

Even Renegades was trying to clean up its act. In 1966 Beckles organised a deputation to ask government for a piece of vacant land on Oxford Street where the band could rehearse. In 1967 he drew up their constitution – a novelty in those days. Both the pan 'tent', today more often called the 'pan theatre', and the constitution are still part of the band.

Men like Beckles, Frank 'Mitch' Baptiste and Jubal Alexander were father figures for the band's youngest recruits, but the Lawbreakers generation was now more mature and they pulled their weight as well. Boldface was a pillar of strength. So too was Small Axe. He got his childhood friend Trevor 'Brutus' Charles to arrange the Renegades' Panorama tunes in 1965, once the Bonapartes left for greener pastures.

Brutus did the job in 1966 and 1967 but he was undependable. An Invaders man, he had many commitments and limited himself mainly to an annual Panorama tune. Otherwise, Renegades' repertoire consisted of a few tunes they had been taught by Junior Pouchet – the leader of the middle-class Silver Stars. Renegades wanted more. It was in a spirit of optimism that they had recently moved their pan tent from the entrance to Harpe Place to Oxford Street, cobbling together a shed from the debris of houses demolished to make way for the redevelopment of the area. This was the context in which they turned to a young Indian teacher named Selwyn Mohammed.

**1962 was the last time that steelbands participated in the biennial 'Trinidad Music Festival'. A 'Music Steelband Festival' was organised in 1963 to celebrate the first anniversary of the nation's Independence and the next year, in June 1964, the National Association of Trinidad and Tobago Steelbands (NATTS) created its own separate competition. Similar festivals were held in 1965, 1966, 1967, 1968, 1972 and 1973, sometimes associated with the celebration of Independence, sometimes as purely musical events. The momentum then faded but in 1980 the competition was revived under a new name, 'Pan is Beautiful Too'. Generally abbreviated in the steelband community to 'The Steelband Festival', it has since been held under different names as a regular biennial event, except for a few lapses.*

Renegades, Carnival 1964, portraying 'Barbarian Hordes'. Photo: Chan's Photographers, courtesy of Gary Chan.

Renegades' mas

In the sixties, steelband's golden years, before the electronic sound systems took over with their louder volume, the steelband movement ruled the streets on Carnival day. Not only did steelbands provide music for masqueraders: their sailors or soldiers or Ju Ju warriors, or whatever masquerade took their fancy, outnumbered the traditional big bands. Through the Carnival masquerade, then, steelbands were embraced by their communities of supporters and members who perhaps never played pan. People from the neighbourhood danced to the music of their band. Pushing the racks of pans through the streets was a mark of pride for young men. And in case of trouble the fighters were there.

John John moved with Tokyo and Fascinators. Upper Laventille came down the hill with Desperadoes. Belmont was with Rising Sun, Woodbrook with Invaders, the middle class with Dixieland and Silver Stars, St James with their many steelbands one behind the other. Even the small Renegades, shunned by many people from their immediate neighbourhood, had their out-of-town supporters from Arouca and El Dorado. And for two years they had the support of Wilfred Strasser, one of Trinidad's great veteran mas designers. Strasser lived in Oxford Street and was responsible for many of the costumes of 'Barbarian Hordes' and 'Fall of the Roman Empire'.

The end of the Badjohn era

Selwyn Mohammed and his brother Bobby were the driving force behind Cavaliers from San Fernando – musically one of the leading bands in the country at the time. It was their victorious sound in 1965, with its overpowering bass section, three times larger than any other band's, which shaped the modern steelband.

One day in November 1967, the same year Cavaliers won Panorama for the second time, Mohammed waited at the airport for Bobby, who was returning with the National Steelband from the Commonwealth Arts Festival in England. Renegades were playing at Piarco Airport to welcome home the team on which they proudly had one member – Randolph 'Baba' St Louis. Mohammed fell into conversation with Jubal, the Renegades captain, who mentioned that he needed an arranger. Mohammed offered his services. About two Sundays later he was working with Renegades.

He wasn't the only new member. In a time of growing discontent among youth, new members were attracted to the steelbands without regard for their stigma of illegality. In the case of Renegades, several arrived between 1965 and 1970 who were to play leading roles, including Patrick Penco, Andy Duncan, John Lopez, Nigel Seales and Randolph 'Baba' St Louis.

Selwyn Mohammed in front of his house in San Fernando. Photo circa 1968, courtesy of Bobby Mohammed.

Still, in 1967 the band was small. 'It had just about ten players – and they only knew two or three tunes. We started right away on a Panorama tune, "Miss Tourist", says Mohammed.

By December 1967, when the Panorama players arrived, the band had expanded to about 30 players, and Mohammed brought along Cavaliers' tuner to make more pans. The tuner was Bertrand 'Butch' Kellman who, as a member of the National Steelband, had already grown close to Baba.

Kellman tuned the pans for free and immediately the improvement was discernible. 'We had only eight tenors', recalls Mohammed. 'I had to beat drums but we also learnt four tunes for the road.'

In 1968, as in every year of the Panorama competition so far, Renegades was knocked out in the first round, but this time many felt they deserved better. 'Robbery with V' headlined a newspaper. They also came third with 'My Heart and I' in the popular Bomb competition wherein bands on the road played foreign music to calypso tempo. The idea behind the 'Bomb' was for one's music to be so innovative as to blow away other bands. As in other competitions, musical rivalry was a substitute for fighting.

Renegades' confidence in Mohammed was not only due to his musical accomplishments. It was also because on the Sunday before Carnival, when Boldface and the other fighters set out to destroy the pans of All Stars, one of whose members in a rumshop brawl had slashed a Renegades man, Mohammed rode with the warriors. And when they were edged out of Panorama preliminaries, he wept. That Carnival Renegades and Cavaliers paraded Port of Spain together.

Mohammed's stint with Renegades was brief – from late 1967 to 1970. But it bridged its transition into a more musically competitive, less destructive organisation. Throughout 1968 he maintained a permanent stage side, travelling from San Fernando every day to hold practice sessions. Renegades' repertoire expanded to about 35 tunes. The band grew. Mohammed introduced a few tenor players from Couva and a few more from Point Cumana. Paramount Films – which had been a sort of sponsor in a low-key way, hiring the band to play in cinemas at movie premieres – began to take a greater interest.

The Trinidad and Tobago National Steelband at Expo 67 in Montreal, Canada. The three men to the right in the middle row are (left to right) Gordon Barrow from Scherzando, Randolph 'Baba' St Louis from Renegades and Bertrand 'Butch' Kellman from Maestros. Photo courtesy of the Information Division of the Office of the Prime Minister.

The band was also encouraged by Tripoli, a top band from the west of the city, whose captain Hugh Borde was close to the Renegades captain. Tripoli was flying high in those days and much in demand for parties and shows; whenever possible they took along Renegades.

Theirs was a remarkable transformation that could not have been accomplished without considerable organisational discipline and respect for the band's hierarchy; but with the backing of authority figures such as Boldface, Mohammed asserted his authority. Once he sent away Small Axe for fooling around on the congas, and the following day that fearsome Lawbreaker returned to ask politely whether he could play tenor. Another time Mohammed ordered Billy 'Whitey Kincaid' Stanley – a man of no small violence – to go home and practise rolling on his dining table. Whitey had come with a cutlass to fight the drummer but he meekly turned around and left.

Nigel Seales first played mas with City Syncopators before joining Renegades in 1965, about the time when he landed his first job at WASA (Water and Sewage Authority). Assistant secretary in 1968, vice-captain from 1971 to 1972, he left the band to join Starlift in 1973 but came back to Renegades in 1981 and has since then been actively involved in the band's leadership. Although he is no longer a member of the stage side, he still plays double seconds at Panorama. Photo 1997.

The National Steelband

The first national steelband was really the 1951 Trinidad All Steel Percussion Orchestra (TASPO). Eleven of Trinidad's best panmen were selected to represent the country at the Festival of Britain, and the results were revolutionary. Under the musical direction of police bandmaster Lt Joseph Griffith, TASPO's pans were expanded to create the first fully chromatic steelband.

It was just a one-off affair, though. An attempt a few years later to form another TASPO to visit Florida was aborted at the last minute by a hurricane which hit the US. And it was in 1963 that the government came up with the idea of forming an official National Steelband.

Prime Minister Eric Williams on a trip abroad had heard a steelband play the national anthem. Williams vowed to show the world what steelband was about. He told the Steelband Association to form a national steelband, emphasising it must comprise the best from each steelband. Not even second best was good enough.

About 30 were chosen. All, including Williams, who was the band's patron, agreed that the pans had to be tuned by Ellie Mannette of Invaders. The Association had a budget of a few hundred dollars for the job. Mannette, however, though enthusiastic about the project, valued his services more highly. He demanded $1,500.

Perturbed, Steelband Association president George Goddard returned to Williams.

'So what?' said Williams. 'Nothing is too much for the culture.'

Fitz Blackman, 'The Bespoke Tailor', was contracted to sew their jackets bearing the coat of arms on their pockets. 'We getting pants, too?' asked Robbie Greenidge, then a talented short-pants boy from City Kids in Belmont.

'You feel the steelband is your father?' retorted Goddard.

The band practised thrice weekly in an old customs shed on the docks. (Members derived great amusement from the two policemen stationed nearby who had to jump to attention every time they rehearsed the national anthem.) But no one was paid a cent, not even the Tobagonians who had to live in Trinidad. The Government adamantly refused Goddard's request that they be paid the same as police bandsmen. The only incentive was the promise of tours. Accordingly, the drop-out rate was high.

Their first tour was to Jamaica, whose rastas they thought were lunatics.

Next the band was invited to the Moral Rearmament Association's (MRA) international youth conference, whose Caribbean section was led by West Indies cricketer Conrad Hunte. The MRA wasn't paying their passage to Michigan, though, so the Association had to pass the cap around to foot the $10,000 bill. One player's mother was so excited she pawned her jewellery to contribute.

All in all, the National Steelband went on three big tours: the 1964 MRA tour, the 1965 Commonwealth Arts Festival tour to the UK, and the Expo '67 tour to Canada. Each time the band lost members. Top panmen remained abroad, men such as Kelvin Hart from City Syncopaters, Clifford Alexis from Stereophonics (who subsequently became co-director of the first university steelband in the US established by G. Allan O'Connor at Northern Illinois University), Desmond Hernandez of Melodies, Errol Zephrine of Starlift and many others.

The politically influential Desperadoes, after complaining of being sidelined, were sent to the 1966 Festival of Negro Arts in Dakar, Senegal. By 1968 the National Steelband was relegated to perform at the opening of government housing estates such as Diamond Vale and Morvant. Shortly thereafter, the old customs shed where the band practised was demolished. And the National Steelband, which no longer interested Williams, ceased to exist.

'Whitey became one of the smoothest players – they was a nice group of fellas, very respectful. They were very serious in the panyard where we didn't even allow smoking,' says Mohammed. 'Even the fellas just out of jail were so.'

And in the Carnival of 1969, they made it for the first time into the Panorama finals. Then on J'ouvert Morning (the pre-dawn opening of Carnival) their rendition of 'In A Monastery Garden' won them first prize. The popular auctioneer A.M. Querino gave the band a $2,000 overdraft and uniforms.

Things were looking up. Renegades went on their first tour that year. An earlier plan to carry 45 players to New York caused a break with the sponsors, Paramount, and then fell through, but George Beckles was able to organise another tour. The band left in October for three months performing in clubs in Europe and North Africa. When they returned on New Year's Eve, it was to a Trinidad roiling in discontent and demands for black power.

Young black men and women, fists in the air, protested in their thousands against the injustices of the society, its racism and unemployment, its skewed value systems and continued domination by foreign multinational corporations. Their cause was joined by militant trade unions and on 21 April 1970, the day on which a general strike was to be launched, a state of emergency was declared by the state and a dusk-to-dawn curfew imposed. Junior ranks in the army mutinied at their remote Chaguaramas base in sympathy with the radicals, and on that same turbulent morning a Renegades team was bused to the airport to embark for Spain on the band's second tour.

First tour, 1969. In front, Andy Duncan. Left to right, second row: Randolph St Louis, Glen 'Wacker' Sandiford, Ronny Williams. Standing behind, left to right: Selwyn Cupid, Dany Grant, Daniel Andrew, unknown (not a band member), Clifford Alleyne, Michael James and John Lopez. Photo courtesy of Andy Duncan.

In those heady days things moved fast. Before they returned a few weeks later, negotiations had already been started and an agreement finalised by Beckles, Boldface and Nigel Seales for a large oil company to sponsor the band, which would henceforth be known as the Amoco Renegades Steel Orchestra.

Supporters celebrate Renegades victory. Panorama 1997. Courtesy of **Newsday**.

3

The road to success

NOTICE
NON-PLAYERS ARE
NOT PERMITTED
BEYOND THIS POINT
By MANAGEMENT

Panorama rehearsals, 1997.

Playing 'Sweet Pan' by Kitchener, Panorama finals, 1984. Photo by Noel Saldenha, courtesy of the ***Trinidad Guardian.***

Playing 'Pan Earthquake' by Kitchener, Panorama, 1994. Photo courtesy of the Information Division of the Office of the Prime Minister.

The art of tuning

Bertrand ‘Butch’ Kellman

Musical instruments can be divided into the traditional and the modern. Traditional instruments, pre-dating the Second World War, are acoustic; modern ones are electronic. The steelpan, however, straddles both worlds. Invented and elaborated in the middle years of the twentieth century, it is resolutely modern. Its basic raw material, oil drums made of steel, is the detritus of industrial society. Yet in its handmade fabrication the steelpan harks back to an earlier time when the functional beauty and genius of a civilisation was the product of its craftsmen.

Bertrand 'Butch' Kellman, 1997.

The first generation of great steelpan tuners, Ellie Mannette, Neville Jules and Tony Williams, wrought their invention in the forties and fifties with an almost aggressive ambition to perfect this new instrument. Those were the years when steelbands competed musically as much as they fought physically. The generation of tuners which followed did its work in a different spirit, however: the spirit of curiosity.

By the time the 16-year-old Kellman hammered his first tenor pan in 1963 to find out how it worked – putting it irreparably out of tune – he already had an inkling. Two or three years earlier, once the sound of a neighbour's pan had turned his ear, Kellman began tuning small grapefruit juice cans, one note per can, a dozen cans encased in a box, until he had made enough for himself and his friends to play simple tunes.

He then joined Southern Marines steelband in Marabella, about three miles from his Pointe-à-Pierre home, and got his first proper tenor pan. 'Playing a pan and being inquisitive you end up pounding that pan', he says. 'You want to find out how it work, so I decide to get a drum and try something.'

As with every other tuner, however, Kellman started off mainly as a pan player, and a good one at that. From 1963, when he was 16 years of age, he played tenor with Southern Marines. Although the band was in decline, in 1965 Kellman was selected to join the prestigious National Steelband. He continued playing with Southern Marines, all the while striving to tune better and better pans. In 1966 he tuned for his first band when Southern Marines' captain and tuner Milton Lyons broke an arm in an accident and Kellman had to make the band's pans.

'Nobody teach me, I make mistakes and errors and most of all listened to Tony Williams and Alan Gervais', says Kellman. 'I'd listen to how their pans sound. You come across a Gervais tenor and you listen to it and pattern what you doing off that. Our pans sounded flattish compared to theirs.'

'I was scared because of their reputation'

In no time he was doing a little tuning for other bands, starting with Texaco West Stars down south, then Dixieland up north, where he branched out to Silver Stars and to Harmonites, in which he met Gervais.

Alan Gervais from Point Fortin was one of the great first-generation tuners. He possessed a gift for tuning high-quality, long-lasting pans with an assembly-line speed. Unfortunately, he drank himself to an early grave. By the late sixties his binges made him unreliable, and Harmonites and Casablanca turned increasingly to Kellman for their instruments. 'Alan didn't use no harmonics. His pans were straight octave pans, loud pans, like All Stars' pans', says Kellman. 'No frills in the note – an A is an A. Harmonics get it weaker.'

In the National Steelband Kellman met two men who would open important doors for his career. The first was Randolph 'Baba' St Louis from Renegades. Baba had a tenor pan made by Wallace Jackman and Kellman bet him he could make a better one. After he did so, Renegades' captain Jubal, and their arranger Selwyn Mohammed, asked Kellman to tune for Renegades. That was in 1968 and Kellman has tuned for them ever since.

'I was scared because of their reputation – if you do something you get clout', admits Kellman. 'So you try to do things the proper way, although once it had problems when they ordered pans late and Boldface and Eddy Boom started to get on bad. Now I understand the band and it's always better to have one tuner who could handle everything instead of two or three – that could create problems.'

Another important contact Kellman made in the National Steelband was Gordon Barrow, a guitar pan player from Scherzando steelband. Barrow liked the tone of Kellman's tenors and asked him to tune for Scherzando. There Kellman met Jit Samaroo, who in turn invited him to tune the instruments for the Samaroo Kids. Thus he became the Samaroo band tuner, travelling with them to keep the pans in tune, much as he does today with Renegades.

'As a player I was listening to anything good, hoping to learn something', recalls Kellman. 'I saw the work Jit was doing – he plays trumpet and keyboard too.'

Renegades arranger Selwyn Mohammed was drinking heavily so Kellman persuaded the band to try Samaroo. They didn't want him to do their Panorama arrangement, though. 'It took plenty talking before they said OK', says Kellman. 'He was scared but I told him if I could make it he could too.'

Renegades panyard. Photo by Norman Magden, 1997.

Kellman was playing for three steelbands: Southern Marines; a small splinter group called Scarlet Symphony; and the National Steelband. Southern Marines was moribund, however, and the days of the other two were numbered. Kellman stopped playing permanently in favour of tuning, which he had decided was more challenging. 'It was nicer than playing – getting good notes on a pan, having the band sound good and knowing that you did that', he says.

'Long time we had an Invaders sound, because our tuners came from the west', reflects Andy Duncan, former Renegades' captain. 'Once Butch found his own sound his tenors sounded different – on the classics they sound better on the higher register, more orchestral on the violin parts like in "Mars" by Holst.' At the Steelband Festival in 1984, Renegades was adjudged to have the Best Tuned Pans.

Despite Duncan's accolade for his tenors, if Kellman has a particular affection for any pans it is for the mid-range cello pans and the bass – which accords perfectly with Jit Samaroo's unusual emphasis on these sections of the band. 'I like a nice cello, it has a good range from G on the bass clef to B flat', he says. 'Tenors are nice but I think a good cello is the best.'

Kellman tunes for other steelbands, of course, including some other leading bands in Trinidad, such as Phase II and Desperadoes,

Renegades panyard. Photo by Norman Magden, 1997.

as well as bands in the US, England, Japan and other Caribbean islands. And he still maintains the connection with Southern Marines, his first band. His workshop – a long narrow shed with a high roof and walls lined with untouched oil drums and racks of incomplete pans – is behind Southern Marines' panyard, where it all began.

Likewise, Kellman continues with the Renegades after twenty years, tuning and blending all of the band's instruments, touring with them for this purpose. The vast majority of tuners specialise in high, mid-range or background pans, some even in blending alone, requiring bands to hire several tuners. Kellman's lack of specialisation makes for a greater uniformity of the sound of Renegades' various sections. Samaroo, for one, considers this a key element in their successes. But it works both ways, because tuning for them and touring with the band makes Kellman part of the Renegades family. And if his efforts contribute to their successes, so too their successes are his.

'Every drum is a different challenge'

The first panmen generally tuned their own pans, if tuning it could be called. A few knocks here with a stone to produce a lump, some more there to get another lump, until the paint can ping pong was able to give you three or four different sounds. The larger du dup was even simpler, its circular face divided along the diameter to provide a two-note bass rhythm.

In 1945 tuning was already becoming a specialised craft. By 1951, after TASPO returned from the Festival of Britain, the modern steelpan in all its essentials had been invented. Tuners were master craftsmen and not every band had one. Throughout the entire country there were no more than two dozen, the greatest of whom was Ellie Mannette, later a professor at West Virginia University. Today there are hardly more master tuners in the world than then, and most of them are in Trinidad.

'It requires good hearing and patience', says Kellman. Actually, it requires more than that. It also takes the knowledge and instincts of a Sherlock Holmes, because nothing is so elusive as a fugitive note on a piece of cold steel.

Tuning here is a misnomer. The word calls to mind what you do with, say, a guitar or a piano. That is, twist a knob which tightens or slackens a string. 'Tuning' a pan really means making it from scratch. Using the word in this sense we can say that Antonio Stradivari was a violin tuner.

There are several stages in the process. First, the face of a 55-gallon steel drum is pounded down to make a smooth bowl whose depth varies according to the particular pan being made. The higher the notes, the deeper it must be sunk. A modern tenor pan – which is actually in the soprano range – goes nine inches down, whereas a bass is not deeper than five inches. This first step stretches the steel and makes it pliable.

Second, the notes are drawn on the face of the bowl, and are pounded out from inside the drum, to create gentle bulges. This is called backing, and the higher the tone the smaller its bulge.

Third, a softened groove is chiselled around every note, to reduce the transfer of vibrations from one to the other.

Nothing is easier than tearing the steel, yet all of this has to be done without leaving hammer marks which would interfere with the uniform vibration of the notes.

1

2

5

6

1) Sinking; 2) Drawing; 3) Backing; 4) Grooving; 5) Burning; 6) Coarse tuning; 7) Fine tuning; 8) Blending: for this final tuning Kellman uses an electronic strobe that measures sound frequencies with far greater accuracy than the human ear is capable of.

'The hammering during the sinking and the backing has made the surface of the pan stretched and soft', explains Swedish acoustic physicist Ulf Kronman in his book *Steel Pan Tuning*. 'The grooving and the backing has also forced local tensions into the metal. Before tuning the pan has to be hardened and the tensions have to be removed. This is done by first heating the metal and then cooling it.'

After that stage of 'burning' the pan over an open fire to temper the steel comes the task

3

4

7

8

easiest to describe and most difficult to do: the actual tuning of notes. In itself this has different stages: 'coarse tuning' to soften the metal and put in the right pitch; 'fine tuning', when pitch and timbre are adjusted; 'tightening' the notes so they aren't easily put out of tune by vigorous playing; and 'blending' when the pans, having been chromed, are tuned and 'blended' with the sound of the other pans of the steelband.

All drums produce different tones, and this is especially important in the case of African talking drums and Indian tabla drums. But the steelpan is the only drum that can produce separate musical notes which are capable of playing melodies.

Guided by a sort of aural sensitivity and intelligence, even the tuners themselves cannot rationally explain their feel for what it requires to tune a particular note on a particular instrument. One reason for this has to do with what is known as the harmonics or partial overtones of musical notes.

Every note you hear on an instrument, say a guitar, is composed of the fundamental note – a C note for example – along with several other specific notes known as partials. The partials harmonise with the fundamental note and allow us to identify the particular timbre of the C – that is, what kind of instrument is playing the note – and its brightness.

How important are these partials? If you likened a musical note to a drawing of a person, the fundamental would be the outline of the figure, and the partials the colours and shades. Thus, even without the figure's outline, your mind would recreate its shape from the chiaroscuro.

When you tighten or slacken the guitar string to get the fundamental note, all the rest, the dozen-odd partials, harmonise automatically. That is, you tune the fundamental note and all the rest fall into place.

Not so with the pan. The fundamental note on a pan is tuned first, and then its modulated partials have to be tuned separately. How this is actually done has to be rediscovered anew by every tuner for every note on every pan. The tuner taps this part of the note, taps that part, trying to get a particular sound, moving the fundamental, shifting first the octave partial (that is the same note only higher, the way a man and a woman could sing a similar note but an octave apart), working then on the various other partials, moving one higher, pulling another lower, until they 'marry' at the right spot.

'Every drum is a different challenge', says Kellman. 'No steel is the same so you can't always get a note by the same method. You have to find alternatives. I may tell another tuner "This note giving me pressure" and he get it right away – I don't know how.'

This is why the world of tuners is full of secret or idiosyncratic techniques. Mostly, however, this world is full of long hours of intense concentration, exploring the mystery of how a single recalcitrant piece of steel can be made to sing, and thus become a full member of the great family of musical instruments.

Jit Samaroo directs, Renegades panyard. 1997.

The arranger

Jit Sukha Samaroo

Coming from a small, rural community whose culture was partly Hispanic, partly Indian, experiencing music through a tiny family band, Jit Samaroo was a stranger to both the urban milieu of the Renegades and the challenge of a big-band Panorama arrangement. For their part, the Renegades were still struggling to acquire the musicianship that the top bands had long perfected. Yet when Samaroo's increasingly complex musical vocabulary, which embraced a study of classical music, encountered the Renegades' singlemindedness, the fusion sparked. Then the precise intelligence of Samaroo's compositions was fired by the passion of the Amoco Renegades.

In the pan theatre, 1997. The blackboard lists the players selected to go on the next tour.

That evening in 1971 when Renegades secretary Nigel Seales met his band's new arranger for the first time at the corner of Charlotte and Park Streets, he wondered if this skinny little Indian man could arrange anything.

In his incredulity Seales epitomised a century of uneasy race relations between lower-class urban Afro-Trinidadians and lower-class rural Indo-Trinidadians, each comprising slightly above 40 per cent of the population, each represented since the 1950s by its own racially based political party. Steelband was an Afro-Creole invention that was largely ignored by Indians (with noteworthy exceptions such as Selwyn and Bobby Mohammed), whose musical culture and social relations were sharply divergent.

Yet Jit Samaroo had been invited to do some work for Renegades on the recommendation of their tuner Butch Kellman. That first night he arranged for them 'One Big Apple' by the Osmond Family. If some were less than impressed, and joked afterwards about 'One Bad Apple', others were optimistic. Later, when Samaroo walked down Charlotte Street to get a taxi home, a group of Renegades accompanied him. Within days they persuaded Boldface, the skipper, to let Jit arrange for both the stage side and Panorama.

Today Samaroo still strikes you as an unlikely arranger for a group such as Renegades, and not only for being Indian in an aggressively Afro-Creole cultural world. Small and delicate-looking, he is unobtrusiveness itself. He speaks softly and with few words, despite having been a professional musician from his teens. His house too is unpretentious, its living room furniture simple. Perhaps this is because Samaroo's personality finds expression in neither words nor material objects but in music.

'I liked music from young. My mother played *dholak*. Indian women played their style of music in weddings', he explains.

Jit Sukha Samaroo was born on 24 February 1950, the sixth of Sukha and Lakia Samaroo's thirteen children. The *dholak* she played is a 20-inch-long horizontally held drum with a playing surface at either end, one larger than the other.

Traditionally, Indian women played the *dholak* alongside other instruments – the harmonium, the *dhantal* – for *laawa* and *maticur* wedding rituals. Those sessions were the traditional Hindu equivalent to today's bridal showers, and the older women made obscene jokes and danced suggestively to a hot, fast music. Thus were young brides introduced to the duties and pleasures of marriage. Men were absolutely excluded from these ceremonies, but boys too young to be left alone at home were allowed, as Jit was on some occasions.

Jit's experience would have thus been unremarkable for a Hindu boy, except that Lakia Samaroo died soon after. Going to wash clothes in the river one morning, she cut her foot on a sharp piece of bamboo. The wound festered and, although she was taken to the hospital, she died, probably of tetanus. That was in 1961, Jit was eleven, and the unexpected loss of his mother was traumatic. It turned him away from Hinduism, which he thought had not adequately helped the family mourn his mother's death. Perhaps it also created an unconscious connection between music-making and the mother he had lost. Certainly it precipitated the creation of a family band.

The learning years

'My big brothers and sisters had gone their way and I was the oldest after my father. I thought if we formed a little group it would keep us together, so we formed a combo – guitar, cuatro, shak shak. We were under the influence of *parang*.'

Jit played guitar. His sister made a little drum from a hollowed tree trunk. A cut hairspray can did duty as a cowbell.

The Samaroos lived in the tiny Surrey (or Suri) Village in the Lopinot valley. Most Indians in Trinidad were concentrated in the sugar-producing plains, but a tiny minority were scattered in the cool highland valleys such as Lopinot where Venezuelan peons of African–Spanish stock had pioneered a cocoa industry. The customs in these isolated pockets were Afro-Hispanic and included the Spanish–Venezuelan tradition of *parang*, in which bands of serenaders would go from house to house singing lively, emphatically rhythmic, Christmas songs. The instruments consisted of guitars, cuatros (a four-stringed guitar), shak shaks (maracas) and a one-stringed bass.

It is not that Jit was any less Indian. He enjoyed the Bombay musicals at Tunapuna's Palladium cinema, like any other Indian youth. But his was a cosmopolitan village, and being naturally open-minded he absorbed its many musical traditions. Not only was there the Venezuelan influence, but when Jit was a child his older brothers Balroop and Kimraj played in a small village steelband. And eventually, after his mother died, he too became interested in pan.

He got a chance to learn the instrument when his neighbour, whose girlfriend lived in Tunapuna near the Scherzando panyard, took him there one evening. 'I met Michael Hamilton there and I taught him to play cuatro', recalls Jit. 'He taught me to play pan.'

Hamilton also remembers that first encounter, which took place around 1965. 'When Jit came to learn pan, he offered to teach me cuatro. Jit was a born panman and in a week he could play like anybody else'.

In Trinidad the steelband movement was dominated by black men plus a more recent handful of middle-class whites and Chinese. Only a few Indians showed an interest in the 1950s. Consequently, Scherzando was unusual in having mainly Indian members such as David Toolsie, Ramdass Sammy and Lal Jagroop, in whose yard the band was located. But the band was not Indian in its music. For that, Sammy, Asgar Ali and others had formed the Saraswatee Steel Orchestra in the early 1950s, which played for Indian weddings and

Foreground: Sonilal Samaroo and his daughter. His son, to the right of a group of cousins, looks at the instrument that kept the family together. The Jets' music room is in the house on the right, one of the four houses the Samaroos built on the land where they grew up. Living in D'Abadie about five miles away, Jit visits Lopinot almost every day, having spiritually never really left the family and the community that shaped him. Photo 2000.

other functions. For Carnival they all returned to Scherzando.

'When we played carols at Christmas, both Indians and Africans came out to jump with us', recalls Hamilton. This was not surprising, for Tunapuna was located at a juncture of sugar-cane farming to the south and cocoa farming to the north, and Indians, Africans and Hispanics lived in easy harmony. It is no coincidence that the only other Indian steelband of the time, Rhythm and Blues, came from another part of Tunapuna. By the time Jit made contact with Scherzando, Saraswatee no longer existed and Rhythm and Blues had already joined Renegades.

From Scherzando Jit carried home a tenor pan and began to teach his younger siblings and they decided to form a family steelband. On 23 August 1967 the Samaroo Kids made their debut at a concert held at the University of the West Indies. The band comprised Jit, Lalchan, Balkissoon, Sonilal, Girly, Pauline and, standing on a box to play the four-bass, Vidya. Their tuner, whom Jit had met in Scherzando, was Butch Kellman.

'It was unusual for Indians to form a steelband', Jit recalls. 'We didn't have much family after that. My father protested a little but not for too long.'

Despite his break with tradition, however, Jit's career has been guided by a very Hindu ideal of the family and its associated concepts of loyalty and continuity. In 1970 the Samaroo Kids (later, the Samaroo Jets) were contracted to play at the Trinidad Hilton, and today, more than thirty years later, they can still be heard there twice weekly playing tunes still arranged by Jit, on pans still tuned by Bertrand 'Butch' Kellman.

'I met Fitzroy Gadjar in Scherzando. He gave us a lot of guidance. He was the Jets' cofounder and manager. He played a great role, him and Butch. He was like a father, friend, pastor. He never got money, it was just for us. Gadjar got us the first performance at UWI for $35. Butch Kellman was the Jets' tuner, adviser and brother.' So if Jit's family became a steelband, the converse held too: the steelband, including Gadjar and Kellman, became his family.

Scherzando metamorphosed into Lever Brothers Canboulay, where Jit met Landig White, their musical director. White realised Jit's potential and encouraged him to help arrange for the band and – unheard-of for a panman at the time – to read music. Fitzroy Gadjar also introduced Jit to Gordon Maliphant, the organist in the Tunapuna

Presbyterian church, who gave him music lessons.

Through his family band Jit became part of the steelband movement, which meant joining in its rituals – in particular entering competitions. The Samaroo Jets entered and won the Religious Music Festival in June 1972. There Jit met Anglican priest Fr John Sewell, a gifted musician and arranger for Tripoli, and with the Steelband Festival coming up in July, he asked Sewell's advice choosing a tune. With Sewell's assistance the Jets got into the finals and Jit won the soloist prize.

More important than winning prizes, however, was the relationship Jit developed with Sewell, who taught him to interpret European classical music. Thereafter the Jets held many concerts featuring Sewell on piano, in Sewell's Point Fortin parish. On every subsequent occasion they entered the Steelband Festival the Jets made it to the finals. Once they came fourth, a considerable achievement given that the other bands had thirty to forty players and the Jets only seven.

But to be a fully fledged member of the steelband fraternity one has to enter the grandest of all steelband competitions, Panorama. And for that Jit needed the larger family which his friend and brother Butch Kellman had persuaded him to join in 1971: the Amoco Renegades Steel Orchestra.

'The main idea was keeping the family together'

Sonilal Samaroo, the youngest member of the Samaroo Jets, has been the manager of the group since 1992. He also plays with a number of other bands in Trinidad.

When we started we were more like a folk group. We'd do limbo, bamboo dance. We would sing with cuatro and guitar. We learned the dances at home, after watching other groups perform. It takes a while for your body to get adapted to limbo, a lot of training and exercising every day. It took practice, but it was not difficult. I used to go down to six and a half inches. I stopped when I was about ten or twelve.

Most of my success is basically Jit's – he taught me most of what I know. He always had the talent to play anything. I didn't decide to play drums. I was six, going into seven. Jit made the decision. It was the same for all of us. We formed, and Jit said who played what. To this day we stuck to it and fell in love with it. Because of my style of playing I got the name 'Killer': 'He's a killer on the drum.'

We are from an agricultural area. Our father was employed as a labourer in the Ministry of Works. He always had a garden and we always helped him, but we never had to hold jobs. We lived in a village. You could give, you could take, so money wasn't important. You could survive even if you didn't do a gig for a week. It was rough but not that difficult. The Presbyterian Church gave a lot of help. We'd perform there every Sunday morning, plus they had bazaars. We also had a lot of functions, annual concerts.

Front row, left to right: Pauline, Girly and Vidya with Sonilal. Back row, from the left: Gordon Maliphant, Jit, Balkissoon, Lalchan, and Fitzroy Gadjar. Photo 1970–71, taken on the verandah of the house occupied by the Maliphant family. Courtesy of Gordon Maliphant.

The main idea was to keep the family together. It was fun and hard work, but we never gave up. In these years there were a lot of family groups; the Jackson Five, the Osmonds. We didn't know where pan would go, but Jit had the foresight that pan would make it big and that we should go into classical music. Steelbands played classical music only for the Festival. To have it permanently on your repertoire was unheard of in the early seventies. We are the only group to have recorded full works from composers, not just a movement. The angle we take is different. We've done a lot of chamber music, because of the size of the band.

Sonilal 'Killer' Samaroo.

The Samaroo family at the Hilton in 1971. Left to right: Lalchan, Jit, Girly, Pauline, Sonilal and Balkissoon. The small Samaroo Kids steelband eventually became a full-time job for several members of the family, which would have been impossible with a larger traditional steelband. The Samaroo Jets is still the only fully professional steel-band in Trinidad.

From the Samaroo Kids to the Samaroo Jets

In 1969 Gordon Maliphant was Head of Citrus Research at the University of the West Indies. He was also choir master and organist at the Aramalaya Presbyterian Church, where the Samaroos worshipped after their conversion to Christianity.

During the late 1960s my wife and I knew of the Samaroos as a young family whose mother had died when Sonilal was only three months old. At that time the Samaroo Kids, as they were called, gave concerts at various events.

The members of that band were Jit and Lalchan on tenor pans, Balkissoon on double seconds, Girly on guitar pan, Vidya on bass pans and Sonilal on the drum set. Their home was a family house with no electricity. Water was collected from a nearby standpipe. There was a verandah with a galvanised roof, where the band practised.

My first real meeting with the Samaroos was to help them finish off 'Voices of Spring' by Johann Strauss. After that I spent many happy hours with the band up to the time I left Trinidad in 1971.

It was felt that it would be beneficial if each member of the band could read music. Jit took a correspondence course in music from Wolsey Hall, Oxford, England. Unfortunately, he failed the exam – largely because he knew too little about the lives and music of individual musicians. That did not worry him one bit. He had gained an insight into the ways in which music works and could be manipulated. He proceeded to employ his new knowledge both in arranging Trinidad music and also in understanding music from other countries. During the same months the rest of his band was learning to read music and eventually they started to learn parts of Schubert's 'Trout Quintet' for piano and string quartet, primarily from printed music.

The superb expertise of Jit Samaroo can be illustrated by the following story. In 1971 a Canadian physical education expert wished to make a 'keep fit' record to use when he returned to Canada. He asked Samaroo for help with a particular exercise. Within 25 minutes, having watched a demonstration of the exercise, Jit composed a suitable piece to fill the correct number of bars, with changes of melody as required, and arranged it for his brothers and sisters. It was recorded straight away.

Jit showed another tremendous ability. If he came to our home in Warner Street for a meal, and we would have some music in the background, he would frequently stop eating in order to listen. When he then went back to Lopinot by car he would be very quiet. Within a few days he could mentally bring back the music he had listened to, arrange it for the rest of the band, and teach them to play it. So within a week a new piece of music was added to their repertoire without anything being written down.

Another aim of Jit was to link the steelband with other instruments. As a result he made experiments augmenting his band with flute, trumpet, solo voices, choirs and piano. His successes in this field are well illustrated by the recordings made by the Samaroo Jets in the years since 1971.

Gordon Maliphant.

'They were very disciplined'

Fitzroy Gadjar was a teacher in Tunapuna and played with Canboulay, a local steelband, where he met Jit Samaroo.

When we were playing in Canboulay, I had a little red car and I'd drop Jit up Lopinot. He was poor, he made his livelihood by gardening and he would walk from Tunapuna to Lopinot after practice, so I'd drop him home. He told me he had brothers and sisters and they had some pans but not a full range. I was secretary of Canboulay, so we got pans for them.

In 1967 Jit asked me to become manager of the band. My wife attended a family life seminar at the university, and on the last day they wanted some fellas to sing and read poems, so I asked Jit to do something. In a week he had about five tunes ready. I remember that Sonilal was so small his foot could hardly reach the pedal to kick the drum. The performance was a resounding success. They passed the hat and they got a big contribution.

So they went on. I was a member of the Presbyterian Church. I found them little gigs here and there, until Holly Betaudier got a contract for them at the Hilton where he had a show running all the time for the tourists. People were coming from all around to hear us. We played for birthday parties, and for the embassies. Once the president of Amoco wanted a small band and he took us, not Renegades.

As a budding pan group the band wasn't proficient in the art of pan yet. Jit's arrangement made the difference: you heard the tenor playing solos and counterpoint melodies. Still that wasn't enough, so they had to put up a show, they had to do bamboo dance, limbo, *parang* music. Jit is a good cuatro man, and they have a good feel for the *parang*. So we'd put an act together. It was tough on the girls. After that bamboo dance they were really sweating.

They were very disciplined. It wasn't a steelband, it was a family. When you say practice, it's practice. They start at 8 a.m., eat lunch, practice, dinner, then practice. That's how they became so proficient.

Tunapuna Presbyterian church where the Samaroo family and Fitzroy Gadjar worshipped, and where Gordon Maliphant played the organ when he met Jit Samaroo. 'We played in a lot of churches', says Jit. 'We still do. We play for anybody of any religion, not just Presbyterians. We've played in Hindu temples. If we have to fast before, we do so.' Photo mid-1960s, courtesy of Gordon Maliphant.

Lalchan, the other tenor in front with Jit, he played since he was a little boy. Jit used to bring him to Canboulay to beat. They had to put two tyres on the ground so that he could reach the pan. He grew up on the tenor.

We entered the Music Festival regularly, we only missed one, and every time we were in the finals. Most times, I played. I was on the guitar and if a part was too difficult for me, Jit would put it on the next pan.

Gordon Maliphant gave Jit the push he needed. Jit had arranged 'Voices of Spring' and I approached Maliphant for help. He said he didn't know anything about pan but he agreed to listen to the group. There were certain things Jit could not understand because of his lack of knowledge, but when Maliphant saw the physical conditions in which the family lived, his heart went out to them. They were so cheerful despite their economic situation. When Maliphant went home, he sent a message saying: 'They have won me over'.

He taught Jit at home, he taught him the whole syllabus and exposed him to the great composers. He'd bring out music from England for him, and Jit caught on very nicely. One day the band played a piece of music for Maliphant in church, and Maliphant asked who did it; he called every musician. He had no idea that it was Jit.

Fitzroy Gadjar.

Jit Samaroo shows a Renegade player how to play a passage. Fitzroy Gadjar recalls Jit teaching him in the same idiosyncratic way: 'I used to play the double guitar or triple guitar and this is how we became friends. We were playing a simple tune and I was at the guitar. When they started to change chords Jit saw that I was in trouble. He stood in front of the pan on the wrong side of the pan and he played the whole tune'. Playing in that position requires unusual ability, because on the pan right and left and up and down are reversed.

The Amoco Renegades

Jit began working with the Renegades in 1971. 'I was scared like hell going into a big band – a rough one too – even if they were not a top playing band. But Butch insisted that I could handle it so I went down', he recalls. 'You look at them and stay quiet till you know them and how to treat everybody. I respected them and they respected me. Some had ideas how they'd like the band to sound. I said, "If you want the band to sound like Starlift, call Ray Holman; if you want to sound like Desperadoes, call Clive Bradley".'

It took a decade for the relationship to gel. 'That first ten years, he was doing good music but we didn't understand', says Andy Duncan, who began playing with Renegades a few years before Jit arrived. 'We were still trying to understand him and he to understand us. This year's tune [1997] we did in a short time – if he tried that in 1972, it would have taken a year.'

Their first Panorama together was in 1972 and in 1982 they won the competition for the first time; thus it took a decade for the team to work smoothly. This was not achieved through the annual Panorama, but in the 'Blockoramas' which were popular in the 1970s. A Blockorama is a free outdoor concert held by up to several bands, either on the block of a panyard or at some public venue like the Savannah. By 1975 Blockoramas were being held almost every weekend, and they ensured that the Renegades stage side got continuous practice. Thus the core of the band honed its skills and bonded with Jit into a tightly knit group.

The demise of the Blockoramas came just as Renegades began topping the Panorama. The victories brought offers to tour. The stage side, therefore, continued its year-round rehearsals and became even closer. 'Touring with Renegades is a great experience. You feel a lot of love in the group, you see them enjoy themselves and express themselves on stage. We've won nine Panoramas but on tours it's nicer', says Jit. 'I'm the arranger but also the most senior. I talk to them, give whatever help or advice I can.'

The long engagement of the 1970s would not have been tolerated by most steelbands; and less so, one would think, by Renegades, who had become accustomed to short-term relationships with different arrangers.

Inside the pan theatre. Left to right: Obasi Farai on the tenor, Miguel Lopez, Jit Samaroo playing double seconds. 1997.

Outside the pan theatre, taking a break from practice. 1997.

Perhaps for that same reason they too felt a longing for stability and continuity. 'The question isn't why we stay with Jit so long', Boldface puts it. 'It's why he stay with we.' The answer is simple: his traditional loyalty to the Renegades family and respect for them, most of whom he has now known since they were adolescents. 'I really love those guys', Jit confesses. 'I am proud of them and really love them in my heart.'

Visit the band during a practice session and you will see this relationship at work. Jit doesn't bang on the side of a pan to get the band's attention, as most arrangers do. He claps softly and there is silence. He explains politely what needs to be done and they do it. Yet he is not above taking suggestions from the band, and they are not chary about giving them. 'I feel stronger', he says, 'when the players have an input because if you want to be successful you must have the support of the players – it's our project, not mine.'

This give-and-take relationship was best illustrated when they were rehearsing 'Lara' in 1995. After the judges' comments on the preliminaries Jit wrote a passage specifically targeted for them. It was difficult and some of the band didn't understand it. They complained. 'We have ten minutes', he told the players. 'You take nine minutes and forty seconds – just give me twenty seconds.'

They came first that year.

Jit Samaroo with tenor player Robert Alleyne. 1997.

Jit's adherence to tradition also shows itself in his music. The Jets' repertoire – and that of the Renegades stage side, for instance – comprises standards of pop, easy jazz, bossa nova, light classics, reggae and calypso: forms with which all listeners are comfortable. The two tunes he has composed for the Steelband Festival, 'A Day in Surrey Village' and 'Song of Lopinot', both echo his childhood. 'I never really left Lopinot,' he claims, although he has not lived there since 1980. In his traditionalism Samaroo is matched by Renegades, whose choice of Panorama tunes has been a Kitchener calypso 31 out of 35 times.

It goes deeper than the choice of music, though, down to Jit's approach to expanding less than two minutes of a Kitchener melody into ten minutes of variations for Panorama without ever straying far from the main theme.

'He always deals with the matter at hand', says Duncan. 'Others take some motif and leave the music aside but Jit always deals with the music, expanding it in different ways, adding new aspects without straying from the theme. He's always relevant and faithful to the theme.'

That faithfulness to a theme, and his precise, step-by-step approach to arranging eschews just going with the flow, which has Jit's detractors complaining that his music is unduly formulaic.

'It's like building a house – the foundation is a good tune', he argues. 'Then I plan the ten minutes by the second: the length of the song, how many variations. I know how I'll start, what I'll do and how I'll end. I look to pull out what others wouldn't go for, some strange chords. The normal licks people go for – I stay away from them. I use a lot of middle-range pans. I started with a lot of tenor but we got the four-cellos in the mid-1980s and you had to create music for them. I target over half to the judges and the rest is for the audience. At the end I aim for the North Stand.'*

Every year he arranges a different calypso; the motifs he chooses to elaborate on and how he does so are different. Thus Jit's formula is no less than the formula of talent.

**The North Stand is a temporary structure built on the opposite side of the stage from the Grand Stand for the duration of Carnival. Spectators do not sit in the North Stand (even when there were chairs, people used to stand on them): they are on their feet, beating on cans and waving colours in support of their favourite bands. The audience is generally younger and the mood more participatory than in the Grand Stand, reminiscent of the relation that existed between the bands and the crowds when steelbands played mostly on the road.*

A rich tapestry of sound

Of our leading arrangers, Len 'Boogsie' Sharpe will give you rich textures and a driving syncopation; Clive Bradley, on the other hand, will be as lyrical as possible, with a more melodic approach. Jit Samaroo, whose style is somewhere in the middle of these two, thinks of his music first and foremost as a means to communicate, a link between himself and his listeners: hence the reason for the clarity of his work. He is known to spend considerable time 'weighting' his various motifs and phrases to good effect. Further, because of his desire to highlight instruments other than the tenors, balancing the sound of the sections is also vitally important to his Panorama arrangements. One of the qualities of his music is his ability to orchestrate, and in particular to use the various instruments in a solo capacity. Initially, in steelband arrangements, the melody was carried mainly by the tenor section. Jit Samaroo was one of the first arrangers to use the full range of instruments, interchanging the melody as the spirit moves him.

In a ten-minute Panorama arrangement, as many as five different variations of the calypso melody may be heard. In Renegades' arrangements, usually the first two renditions of the verse are in the tenor line, the first, a faithful representation of the calypso as sung by the calypsonian, and the second, a highly syncopated variation, still in the tenor line. By the third playing, however, Jit often places the melody in a lower instrument, giving it a newness of sound. He is known for using the cello section here to good effect, or even the double seconds or the guitar pans (strumming instruments), which are rarely highlighted. A good example is the arrangement of 'Pan in a Rage' by Winston Scarborough (De Fosto). There, because of the length of the chorus and the 'bridge' in the calypso, the cellos played the melody by the second variation! In 1989 with Winsford Devine's 'Somebody', when Renegades again won the Panorama, Jit had the cellos and the four pans doing a 'counter-melody' (a second melody which sounds simultaneously with the calypso melody). This happened at the first playing of the calypso verse by the tenor. This subtle focus on the lower instruments prepared the listener for the entrance of the second playing of the verse, which he gave to the double seconds.

With this 'passing of the melody' from one instrument to the other, Jit works to elicit maximum sensitivity from all the players. He will have them at times play softer or will find some way to reduce the volume of the counter music [music that should really be an accompaniment to the main musical idea]. I have seen him subdue the tenor section, some of the players standing still, sticks crossed, or increase the sound of the melody by 'doubling' it with, say, the quadrophonic pans, or some other instrument capable of that range. Each playing of the calypso is different in syncopation and presentation. Add to this the various short 'breathing spaces' between the verses, which are called 'bridges', and the free-style, developmental, longer sections called jam sessions – by far the most exciting sections of the ten-minute arrangement – and you have a very rich and complicated tapestry of sound indeed. Jit has the ability to sift and sort all his musical ideas until just the correct balance is achieved. It is a fascinating process, which eventually manifests a carefully orchestrated sound, so that the whole is a perfect fit, melodically, rhythmically and harmonically.

One of Renegades' hallmarks is a fast, crisp tempo with an almost military precision. Under his direction, the band has the ability to momentarily abandon the calypso rhythm in mid-stride so to speak, swing into such rhythms as zouk, chutney, samba, rumba or ring bang, and return again to the calypso rhythm just as adroitly! Jit would use this towards the end of the arrangement, usually in the last 'jam session' as a means of heightening the sense of climax.

He is fearless when writing for the basses. He composes very fast, scale-like passages for his bass line, a challenge for his players because of the considerable overtones

Jit Samaroo, Panorama semi-finals, 1998.

[sound which lingers in the air, blurring the harmonies] of that instrument. He is also adept at 'word painting', using key words taken from the lyrics of the calypso. This is another example of his desire to communicate with his audience. In Lord Kitchener's 'Mystery Band' in 1993, when Renegades again won the Panorama competition, he used the 'Kayamb', an indigenous instrument which he brought back from La Reunion, along with the double tenors, cellos, guitars and the rhythm section, to create the rattling sound of the debris in the river 'coming down'. This was an exciting moment indeed. Similarly in Kitchener's 'Pan Earthquake', at the beginning of the music he imitated the rumbling sound of the impending earthquake: fans at the Savannah erupted with a corresponding roar of approval. When all is said and done, Jit Samaroo is a master craftsman.

Joslynne Carr Sealey

FOR
RENT
bp
Trinidad and Tobago
Thank You
BP Trinidad and Tobago LLC
for your support and partnership thro
the years.
INTERNET.WWW.RENEGADE

Sponsorship matters

The steelband movement did more than create a new form of music. It was an experience of cultural liberation, and after independence it became a cornerstone in the new nation's definition of itself. Throughout the years the state has funded steelband competitions. But subsidising dozens of steelbands was beyond the means of a small country like Trinidad, with a population of fewer than one and a half million people. The corporate sponsorship of bands, initiated at the instigation of the government, played a decisive role. It gave the bands the resources they needed to maintain themselves and evolve into the well-trained, musically competitive ensembles they have become.

Paying for the pans and their racks represents a sizeable investment by the company. Taking care of the instruments, maintaining the panyard, painting and repairing the racks are also an investment, of time rather than money, which is shouldered by band members.

Corporate sponsorship of steelbands began in the fifties when the Esso Oil Company funded a small band, assembled from Southern Symphony players in the south of Trinidad, which became known as the Esso band. However, steelband sponsorship became widespread only in the sixties. By the mid-sixties 26 out of 90 members of the National Association of Trinidad and Tobago Steelbands (NATTS) were sponsored, including top bands such as the Coca Cola Desperadoes, Solo Harmonites, Guinness Cavaliers, Pan Am North Stars, Carib Tokyo, Angostura Starlift, and Esso Tripoli, which left the island on a three-year tour through the United States in 1968, never to return.

The growing complexity of steelband music and the specialisation of professional tuners and arrangers gave sponsored bands an advantage over the unsponsored ones, although there was a wide variation in the financial contribution made by different sponsors. Sponsorship could involve paltry sums indeed – just enough to buy T-shirts for the panmen – but it could be more generous, for it was actively promoted by a subtle arm-twisting on the part of the then Prime Minister Eric Williams.

Williams' was a delicate balancing act in the newly independent republic. On the one hand, sponsorship was calculated to maintain political support for the government in the black working class, which grew increasingly restive as the sixties drew to a close. On the other hand, sponsorship was a kind of tax on the large companies, which were defended by government policies from the claims of trade unions. Some panmen complained of being exploited by their sponsors, of giving far more than they received. But generally steelbands took quickly to sponsorship; panmen were content, proud even, to be associated with high-profile companies.

In 1970 the parties to this social contract fell out. The black power movement and its unemployed youths attacked the government and the capitalist class. The steelband movement in general supported black power, with the notable exception of Desperadoes. Williams responded on two fronts. First, he subverted the steelband movement by encouraging the formation of a Steelband Improvement Committee as an alternative to NATTS. Second, within weeks of the 1970 black power rebellion he increased the pressure on large corporations to adopt steelbands, especially in the hotbeds of discontent such as La Cour Harpe.

It was at this point that the American oil company known as Amoco entered the corporate sponsorship picture. 'The government wanted to deter young people from the black power rebellion and they invited Amoco to sponsor a steelband', says Frank Arlen, Amoco's former Public Relations Officer. Amoco responded positively. The company had just discovered oil off the east coast of Trinidad and was preparing to produce its first barrel. Orvell Gaither, who was President of Amoco Trinidad from 1970 to 1974, remembers the

Signing the contract, from left to right: George Beckles, Lennard 'Boldface' Patrick, Fitzroy McKain for the band and Orvell Gaither for Amoco. The sponsorship agreement was renewable every year and this photo was taken in the early 70s. Courtesy of Frank Arlen.

island as a place filled with music, especially at Carnival time: 'People were beating on jars filled with water, anything'. In the midst of that panoply of sound, the steel drum was an intriguing musical instrument. But it was not an interest in the music that moved Amoco to sponsorship. A company with a budget of half a billion dollars a year had every reason to support the recently established Trinidad and Tobago government. 'It behoved us to do that', explains Gaither; 'we supported Williams' policy of getting the kids off the street and providing a modicum of something constructive for them to do.'

Amoco did not select Renegades. One version of the story is that the band's name was drawn from a hat; another that members of the government suggested that choice. Though the company did consider the presence of Jit Samaroo, 'a young man from a fairly promising Indian musical group', as a plus, it was the fact that Renegades seemed to be, in Gaither's words, 'the most needy of them all' that motivated Amoco to sponsor them. 'They weren't popular. When Desperadoes had 100 players Renegades had difficulty to find 65 – they were a little group in the middle of the stage', recalls Arlen. 'Once they didn't even have canopies.'

The contract, signed in June 1970, was written along traditional lines. The Renegades negotiators drew on the agreement between Starlift and the Canadian Imperial Bank of Commerce. It was the band, not the company, which insisted on adding the Amoco name to its title. 'Renegades wanted to be known as the Amoco Renegades. It was a tremendous source of pride then to have a corporate sponsor of stature. It meant respectability, acceptance and assurance for the future', explains Frank Arlen.

In the beginning the relationship was modest. The company provided T-shirts, pans and wheel systems. It didn't even use the half-dozen free performances the band was contracted to provide. If some charitable organisation wanted a steelband, Amoco would donate Renegades. Amoco's initial attitude can be described as an unusual

Frank Arlen, on stage with the band, Panorama finals 1997. Photo by Lester Forde, courtesy of the ***Trinidad Guardian****.*

What is a panyard? A home for a steelband. A place to store the instruments and to rehearse. A castle, a base, a headquarters. A school. A theatre. A sports club. A recreation club and dance hall. A bar. A steelband without an adequate panyard eventually dies.

In 1992 the company purchased a lot of land on Charlotte Street where Renegades had been rehearsing for years, thus insuring the band's long-term future. The Oxford Street pan theatre had always been too small for the big Panorama rehearsals which first had to be held in the open in the Harpe.

combination of corporate generosity and indifference. Once the company became involved with the band, however, another factor entered the equation: the personal interest of key members of the company in the welfare of the band, such as Cedric Weekes, for instance, who was the Public Relations Officer in the early years, or Frank Arlen who succeeded him. Similarly, every president of the company since 1970 has developed a deep affection for the band.

Gaither himself, who was too busy to devote much attention to the band, remembers going with his driver to the Oxford Street panyard to hear the newly named Amoco Renegades rehearse and to talk to 'the boys'. The band would play for barbecues or seated dinners at the president's home. This exchange was warm enough to extend the Lawbreakers' net of protection over company officials. 'Don't you worry, Mr Gaither', a band member once wrote to Gaither, 'should any trouble ever occur, we'll come to your house and protect you.'

The Powers' years

The Renegades' relationship to Amoco remained steady during the gestation period of the seventies, as the group – showing remarkable patience – solidified the relationships with arranger Samaroo and tuner Kellman. It remained for Bob Powers, who assumed the presidency of Amoco Trinidad in 1980, to create some new momentum. Powers had a long-standing affection for Trinidad, having first come to the island in 1958 for Carnival. He was Chief Engineer for Amoco in New York when Amoco Trinidad was acquired. And when he came to the island in 1979, he established what he calls 'a love affair' between himself, his wife Fiffie, the company and the band, partly as a way of changing the then low morale in the company.

Powers put the band on a firmer contractual basis, not only guaranteeing a fixed income from the company each year, but also offering the counselling services of the company's legal department, to advise the band about appearance contracts and so forth. According to Powers:

> We were looking over their shoulders but not down their throats. We let them know that the company was behind them 100 per cent. They knew how much money they could have each year. We would help them in any way that we could. We actively met the guys and associated with people like Patrick Penco and Jit Samaroo, a true genius. The change in company attitude made them so happy. We gave them confidence that there was somebody behind them to give them what they needed to succeed. I could see it in their eyes, the confidence growing; we believed in them, and I think it mattered.

Powers became President of Amoco Trinidad at a time when the company had stabilised; when it could afford to turn its attention to establishing tennis tournaments and subsidising steelbands. But it was Powers' identification with the band that triggered the change in attitude. Having grown up during the depression, Powers empathised with the poverty of the players. 'Nobody had been as poor as I was. But the kids in the Renegades were almost as poor as Fiffie and I had been during the Depression. It's real good for your heart to see them get an opportunity to make themselves into great musicians. I wish I could have given each of them jobs.' Powers played drums in the panyard; one year he crossed the stage with the orchestra at Panorama time.

His arrival in 1979–80 was timely. Having made it to the Panorama finals for the first time in 1978, Renegades was poised for success. Buoyed by the support from Powers and Amoco, they came third in 1980, second in 1981, and won their first Panorama in 1982. Powers remembers the Panorama victory in 1982: 'It was like a sports event when parents have a child who succeeds; there is terrific pride, a sense of real accomplishment for the child and the parent.' The pride was by then national as well as personal and corporate. According to Mrs Powers, herself a co-architect of the sponsorship policy, the strategy worked for the company as well as the band, helping to lift morale all around and to establish a sense of the common Trinidad identity of both the sponsor and the sponsored during the heady period when steel orchestras were claiming their place in the world arena. In 1980 the Steelband Festival (renamed that year 'Pan is Beautiful Too') was revived, a festival which Powers remembers as 'an experience in which the steelband sounded like a symphony orchestra up there; a truly professional musical affair at which you wore a coat and tie and your wife wore a pretty dress', in contrast to Carnival 'which was fun'.

Photo by Norman Magden, 1997.

Patterns of patronage

Throughout the years Powers helped to establish a paradigm of benign patronage, of oversight without intervention, which proved most successful. It was Frank Arlen, a

Public Relations Officer of Amoco who had been trained as an artist with a career in journalism and an ear for music, who introduced Powers to the musicianship of the Renegades. And it is Arlen who succinctly described the sponsorship as one in which 'the main aim of Amoco as sponsor is to assist the band, whatever the needs and priorities of the band might be, within the framework of a renewable annual contract'.

February 2000: Prince Charles takes a knock in Renegades' panyard. Left to right: Selwyn John, tenor player; Hayden Holder, tenor player; Obasi Farai, tenor player; Prince Charles; calypsonian 'Superblue' (he composed the tune Renegades played that year for Panorama); behind him the Renegades captain, Harold Moses.

Piarco airport, Trinidad, 1997. Amoco Renegades leaves for a tour.

Steelbands have different structures and, thus, different needs. Some bands have more than one tuner; some bands change arrangers from year to year or sometimes have more than one arranger or more than one tuner. In others the arranger and tuner are members of the band and provide in-house services. Thus, each orchestra has to find a particular configuration of sponsorship. In the Renegades' case, the company's assistance extends to all aspects of the life of the band. The company provides instruments, wheel systems and uniforms, for the oversized Panorama band and the stage side. It supplies promotional tools such as T-shirts. It arranges for company-sponsored foreign tours, taking the band, for instance, to Argentina and Houston in 1997. It makes its legal department available to the band for assistance in writing performance contracts. It does not pay players, but it does provide stipends when the band has exceeded the number of free performances that it is required to offer in exchange for sponsorship, or when the company feels that the band has performed or served beyond expectations.

As the band began to grow from its early Panorama size of sixty to sixty-five members to its full present contingent of two hundred, including reserves, it required a larger space. Amoco first leased an abandoned lot on Charlotte Street, and for three or four years, the space was leased for a few months before Panorama. Then the company bought the land, which it holds in its own name, and provided it as a year-round panyard, basically a home for the band. The company has an understanding with the band's leaders, rather than a formal lease arrangement, to provide the space. In return, the band takes care of it, seeing to the pipes, the plumbing, and providing some of their own money and sweat to build food stands and other facilities on the property, creating a locale where band members can hang out as well as play, where the band can host events such as its Friday night concerts of 1995–1996, at which other groups performed. The company also helps to maintain, and would like to develop, the government-owned indoor space on Oxford Street where the band rehearses for its foreign tours and local concerts.

Most importantly, the company also pays the arranger and tuner, Jit Samaroo and Bertrand Kellman. Samaroo receives a monthly retainer; Kellman is paid by the job. They are not band members, but both travel with the Renegades frequently on international tours and both claim pride of place with the band.

In 1998, British Petroleum acquired the Amoco Oil Company and inherited the sponsorship of the band. BP immediately demonstrated its support by financing the formation of a junior orchestra to train the next generation of players. Only the name of the band changed: it is known in the new millennium as the BP Renegades Steel Orchestra.

David Wight, Amoco President (1992–2000) converses with double seconds player Edmund Willis during a party in the panyard. Photo by Arthur Edwards circa 1995.

Sponsorship of steelbands has always been controversial. There are those who claim that it has thrown just enough money to the bands to get them off the streets, without providing the kind of training that might enable band members to earn a living from their musicianship or to develop further (and fully) the orchestral dimensions of pan. Others see the very fact that bands are still composed of players who are for the most part amateurs as one of the strengths of the Trinidad steelband culture. Clearly, Renegades are a happily sponsored band. The only criticism the band will articulate about its sponsor is the occasional tongue-in-cheek charge that the company has made life

Limbo in the panyard. Photo by Arthur Edwards, 1997.

almost too easy: without the struggle for survival, the orchestra must now struggle to retain its competitive spirit.

The company does not make decisions for the players; it does not own the band: it helps, assists, and works with its members. On the matter of instruments, for instance, the company might question a price if it feels it is too high, but it neither orders nor approves the instruments. This attitude is remarkably similar to that of their arranger, Jit Samaroo, who has similarly abstained from any of the internal politics. The result is the unique continuity of a band having the same sponsor, tuner and arranger for a quarter of a century, and if that is not an important ingredient in the band's musical successes, nothing is.

1999: the company's annual pre-Panorama finals party.

Sunshine Snacks
JUNIOR
2000

Panorama finals, 2000. Photo by Pablo Delano.

Antonio Yeates on the bass, Panorama preliminaries, 1995. Photo by Arthur Edwards.

Eyes on the prize

Steelbands thrived on the sense of belonging they gave to members. But even that requires vindication, and here competitive success was important, in mas, in fighting, and finally in musical accomplishment. As steelbands grew larger and louder, their mobility decreased. Since the 1970s their energies have concentrated on a single moment: the Panorama competition. There, on that stage, each band found its annual ten minutes of fame, hoping to transform it into glory.

Shortly before midnight the band is on the track leading to the Panorama stage, a glittering caravan inching through the crowd which has preferred to remain outside the competition and hear the bands taking their last, anxious rehearsals. Photo by Norman Magden, Panorama finals, 1997.

Panorama

At 2 a.m. the crowd in the Queen's Park Savannah is thicker than ever. The old race course pavilion known as the Grand Stand is overflowing. Opposite, the North Stand, a temporary steel structure, bears a rowdier mass of swaying, drumming, drinking humanity. Panorama is in full swing.

In the Panorama steelband competition, each of the country's steelbands presents an arrangement of one of that year's calypsoes before a panel of adjudicators and an enormous, keyed-up, raucous and highly partisan audience. Bands are eliminated through preliminary, zonal (regional), and semi-final rounds, leading up to the finals, Saturday night before Carnival.

Each band is allotted ten minutes at the finals, which constitute the moment for which nearly a thousand panmen or women have been waiting all year. Those ten minutes represent the climax to months of late nights drilling in their panyards, learning to perform intricate musical arrangements, rehearsing over and over their top-speed, split-second timing. It is the only time steelbands bring out all their troops, the full complement of players (120 until it was reduced to 100 in 1999), the supporters, the veterans who no longer play but look on with pride at what they have created.

This all-night show usually begins about an hour late, by which time the space Trinidadians call the Big Yard is already jammed. Anticipation is tangible through the rumble of talk and argument, the shouting and laughter. Miraculously, there are no fights. Loudspeakers blare the calypso which the next band will play. Vendors thread through the seething mass, selling beer. Men are using those same bottles, once emptied, to beat a rhythm with wedding rings, spoons, bottle openers – anything to hand. A louder, syncopated clanging rises from the crowd, pounded out by those who have specially brought along their percussion – car brake hubs – to enhance the loudspeakers' deafening tempo.

The Grand Stand, Panorama finals, 1999.

On stage, Panorama finals, 2000.

On the track leading to the stage, bands are lined in readiness for their turn to perform. Thousands are milling around them. Teenagers are marauding in packs. Older folk stand around drinking, arguing the merits of each band. Players are running through their tunes a last time as the captains and arrangers marshal their forces like generals. The night air is cool but dusty and charged with excitement.

On stage all is frantic. A swirling crowd wheels the fifteen or twenty racks of steelpans into a tight battle formation. Flashbulbs are popping as the band's captain directs the moving racks into position, tenors in front facing the judges, basses on either side, seconds behind tenors – or whatever has been logistically determined by the musical arrangement and the band's instrumentation. Panmen flick their wrists to limber up, or stretch their arms.

Suddenly, silence descends like a curtain. The loudspeakers stop in mid-song. A voice comes across the PA system, announcing the first band, where they are from, their captain, their arranger, the tune they will play, the tuner of their pans. A roar of applause rises briefly as the players bow, and then it dies down. A half-dozen rapid clangs cut through the tension to do the one-two-three. And the band, coiled like a spring, explodes into music.

The criticism of Panorama is legion: the all-night shows are far too long; the competition has narrowed steelbands until many can only play a single tune – the Panorama tune; only large, wealthy bands which could afford top arrangers and tuners have a realistic chance of winning; small bands are thus drained of ambitious players; the push for greater power has made steelbands too large and unwieldy; the music is too complex and has lost its soul; besides, the idea of aesthetic competition is absurd anyway. All of which is partly true but made quite irrelevant by the brute fact of Panorama.

Rivalry has always been the motor of the steelband movement. Long before Panorama existed, from the moment the first steelband came on the streets on Carnival Monday of 1939, rivalry inspired the elaboration of the pan. Tuners, without ceasing to collaborate, also sought to outdo one another, or at least catch up. The man who saw a pan with four notes tried to make one with eight; someone else saw him and aimed for twelve. One band heard another playing an unusual tune on Carnival, and tried to learn something even more impressive to outdo that band the following Carnival.

Panorama finals, 1998.

Top photo: Singer Shanaqua waves the Renegades' flag while the band plays her tune, 'Pan for Carnival'.

Bottom photo: Dexter Bernard on the double tenor.

Whenever two bands met on the streets, each tried to out-play the other, either in skill or volume. And if that did not work, they could always fall back on the older tradition of sticks and stones and bottles.

Apart from such impromptu competitions more formal ones were organised, sometimes by the bands themselves, sometimes by enterprising impresarios. Prizes in the early days were practically worthless: a cheap trophy, a case of rum, a set of dishware. Playing before an audience and winning was sufficient reward.

From 1949 on, a Carnival Sunday night steelband championship competition was held, which became the 'Carnival Bacchanal' show in 1960. It was not successful, though. The top bands earned more by playing at parties than they could win by competing. So in 1963 the government sponsored a new competition whose appearance fees alone equalled what a band could earn, and whose prizes were substantially more. This new competition was called Panorama, and it quickly became the main occasion on which steelbands would show what they could do.

There were other important competitions, of course, such as the Steelband Music Festival and the Bomb competition. In the latter case this hugely popular event saw steelbands on the road seeking to outdo one another in musical innovations by playing diverse types of music to calypso tempo. The

North Stand. Panorama preliminaries, 1998.

The preliminaries

The preliminaries mark the true beginning of Carnival for the pan community. The stages of Panorama have changed many times and continue to do so but as a rule the preliminaries take place two weeks before the finals. In Port of Spain some 35 to 40 bands compete for admission to the semi-finals. (Tobago and the South Zones have their own preliminaries.) This grand display of music starts in the early afternoon and ends in the small hours. Thousands of pan enthusiasts crowd the stage, or stroll among the bands massed around the Savannah in a holiday atmosphere complete with picnics, children and sunshade umbrellas. The 'prelims' have less of the competitive intensity than the finals or the 'semis'. Rather, a perambulating sociability prevails.

Panorama preliminaries, 2001.

results – to hear Mozart for instance, played to a powerful African rhythm – were startling and beautiful. Hence the term 'Bomb', for the band rehearsed in deep secrecy to surprise listeners and devastate rivals.

The three main competitions – Panorama, the Bomb and the Festival – were not as unrelated as they might seem. The classically oriented Music Festival was an inspiration for the Bomb, which began spontaneously in the fifties when Trinidad All Stars, planning to show up Crossfire, secretly rehearsed and performed Beethoven's 'Minuet in G' to calypso rhythms. Thereafter it became regular fare on that competition to hear the classics played to an uptempo jam. In turn the musical understanding gleaned from fusing the classics with calypso – the knowledge of key changes, harmony, counterpoint, chords and broken chords, arpeggios, bridges and obbligatos – fed into the calypso arrangement for the Panorama competition. It is no coincidence that after winning the 1962 Music Festival with 'Voices of Spring' by Johann Strauss, North Stars went to win the first and second Panorama competition in 1963 and 1964. Similarly, it is no surprise that Jit Samaroo, the most successful Panorama arranger, interprets calypsoes for Panorama in a highly ornamented baroque style.

The Bomb competition ended in the 1970s, and although there has been a recent attempt to revive it, that has been with only limited success. The Steelband Festival, on the contrary, has endured, providing over the years a unique opportunity for pannists to explore the possibilities of their instrument. Other competitions have also been created since the mid-1980s, such as the Pan Jazz Festival and Pan Ramajay, both of which are for small ensembles and soloists, and emphasise improvisation. But the competition which has come to almost define the steelband movement is Panorama. If a band doesn't enter Panorama it isn't a real steelband, although there are only three bands which have been in every single Panorama: Desperadoes, Invaders and Renegades.

The steelband equivalent of the Latin American gourdscraper, the scratcher is made from metal and placed in the band's rhythm section. Steelband pioneer Sonny Jones, who makes scratchers for the Renegades, explains: 'I make them to Jit's instructions. You have to use aluminium sheet so they fit between the cymbals and the irons which is the loudest instrument in the band. It have three gauges of aluminium and you get different tones'.

Pushing the racks on stage. Panorama preliminaries, 2001.

Judges at the Panorama preliminaries, 1997. Photo by Pablo Delano. Judges are trained musicians known for their competence and their experience with steelband music. They also need considerable stamina to sustain concentration throughout the exhausting Panorama schedule. Each year the leaders of the bands approve a list of potential judges presented to them by the officers of Pan Trinbago, who then make the final selection.

Conquering the Big Yard

Soon after the arrival of Jit Samaroo in 1971 most members of Renegades were confident that the team was complete. There was a good sponsor, a good tuner, a disciplined, combative organisation, and a promising arranger. In 1972 Samaroo arranged Sparrow's calypso about violence, 'Rope', so that the tenors rolled like sirens. The more discerning players knew he had potential.

All they needed now were good pannists. Boldface, who had replaced Jubal as captain, set about plugging the holes.

He had persuaded the leading tenor players Ronald Alexis and Sterling Sample from a small but established band in St Ann's, Kintups, whose captain he knew, to play with Renegades in 1971. After practice he would see to it that they were dropped home. Every year after that one or two more Kintups joined Renegades, until there were nine or ten of them, some of whom are still playing with the band a quarter of a century later.

Success, however, was a long, steep climb. The early 1970s were difficult years for the band. During the late 1960s Boldface and Jubal, with Beckles' backing, had provided good leadership in a counterpoint manner. Boldface was vice-captain, the rough, strict side of the band's administration, its rigid discipline, while Jubal as captain represented its friendlier, more easy-going aspect. After the 1969 tour, however, Jubal lost the band's earnings. He said that they were stolen, but there were allegations of impropriety. Boldface was made captain in 1971, and the balance was upset. Soon there were complaints about his autocratic leadership.

Lennard, 'Boldface' Patrick, two-times Renegades captain (1971–74; 1991–94), at the Annual General Meeting, 1997, while band members get ready to elect the band's leadership. Older members who don't play with the band any more, but are still actively involved, are key to insuring the organisation's continuity.

The band had a disciplinary committee but players were not paid wages which could be deducted. Like Goldteeth before him, Boldface applied the law in its traditional form. 'I wasn't nobody friend', he recalls. 'You had to be rough. If you come to practice, you come to practice. Long time, if a man playing the fool, you have to rough him up'.

In 1973, he roughed up John Lopez, a long-standing player, in a way many felt was uncalled for. Between 1972 and 1973, a significant number of players left the band. Anthony 'Castro' McQueen and his brother Victor, old Lawbreakers, were the first to walk out. (Castro became Phase II captain.) Nigel Seales joined Starlift where he remained until 1981. Others migrated to Deperadoes or Tokyo. The largest group, which included later Renegades captain Andy Duncan, formed their own steelband in the Harpe, Survival.

Survival was able to bring out a larger mas band than Renegades for Carnival 1974. But Renegades was their first love and they did not want to destroy it. They soon came back. In 1975 Boldface was removed from leadership and Randolph 'Baba' St Louis took over.

These upheavals will perhaps explain Renegades' mediocre performance in the early 1970s. From 1969 to 1972 the band had reached the semi-finals four times in a row. Then the band's performance dropped off.

'So tell dem people/ I am a statue/ In the heart of Town/ I like the way they play/ I like the things they say/ and for '76 J'Ouvert/ I coming down... I coming down.' The Mighty Sparrow.

The statue was that of Arthur Cipriani – a well-remembered labour leader and politician in the 1920s and 1930s – and the tune was about the music and its power to make the statue dance on Carnival day. Having reached the semi-finals, Renegades had high hopes for this Panorama. For more effect they had one of them impersonating the statue. But things did not work out as planned. 'After the zonal finals', says Penco 'Jit had put in some new piece but everybody didn't get it. It was towards the end and that confused the statue when he was supposed to come down, and confuse everybody else too.' This lack of co-ordination was fatal: the band did not make it to the finals that year. Photo 1976, courtesy of Frank Arlen.

For three years they did not go beyond the preliminaries.

They could easily have lost faith in their arranger. 'Some people did not want Jit', explains Andy Duncan, then a young player in the band. 'Jit is East Indian and his timing was different; we don't have quarter notes, our rhythms don't have that, but his background does. So some of the timing of his music was confusing. We had to learn his rhythmic patterns and he had to learn ours'. But they did not walk away from him, nor he from them. 'Before him we had an arranger who would come some nights and not come other nights. Jit came every night. You can't discard somebody like that, and the longer he stayed the more we appreciated his musical capabilities.'

Nevertheless, the lack of success was a strain. Other equally old bands such as Desperadoes had long transformed their combativity into musical proficiency. Even much more recent bands, such as Harmonites, had acquired recognition for their music, while Renegades had to bear the taunt that they could only play Indian music. During these years they would talk for hours after practice sessions, hungering for the day Renegades would be recognised, and defiantly refusing to be dismissed.

'We had to prove we were not in the boundaries they set for us', recalls Duncan. 'We had no recognition yet, we had only made one little tour – ten men on a boat – but when we came back we would talk for hours about making Renegades a household name all over the world'.

Patience was needed. Patience for Samaroo to gain Panorama experience and to understand the culture from which Renegades came, patience for the band to become comfortable with his style of music. In 1976 the band, which used to practise for the competition in the open space behind the Oxford Street pan theatre, rented a lot of land on Charlotte Street. They began climbing the ladder again.

That year they played Sparrow's 'The Statue' and reached the semi-finals with 13 other bands. In 1977, they again made it as far as the semi-finals, and again they got no further. But in 1978 they clawed their way into the finals. It was the first time and their inexperience told: bands that they had bested in the semi-finals beat them into seventh place. The lesson was not lost. The 1979 Panorama was boycotted by most steelbands to demand more prize money, but in 1980 when the competition was resumed, Amoco Renegades came third, in 1981 second, and in 1982, ten years after Jit Samaroo arranged his first Panorama tune for the Amoco Renegades, they won.

1982 Captain Wilfred Cox receives the trophy for Amoco Renegades' first Panorama victory. The brother of Renegades representative on the National Steel Orchestra Randolph 'Baba' St Louis, Cox, who now lives in the US, captained the band from 1980 (after Carnival) to 1983. Photo courtesy of Frank Arlen.

The Steelband Festival

The succeeding years were a time of consolidation when the band gained experience, learning how, for instance, not to let the adrenalin of a finals night accelerate the tempo. It was also a time they ventured into a different sphere, that of classical music.

Samaroo had known John Sewell, an Anglican priest, since the Jets won the Religious Music Festival in 1972. Sewell was a classically trained pianist with a deep interest in pan. He conducted Tripoli, and a close friendship grew between him and Samaroo, who was eager to learn as much as he could about classical music. Samaroo relied heavily on Sewell's advice on the Jets' repertoire for the Steelband Festival.

Steelband Festival 1988. John Sewell takes Amoco Renegades through Gustav Holst's 'Mars, the Bringer of War'. Photo courtesy of the ***Trinidad Express****.*

Sewell's band, Tripoli Steel Orchestra, had ceased to exist by 1971. It had gone on a three-year tour with Liberace, and most of its members never returned to Trinidad. So Sewell channelled much of his pan tabanca into assisting the Samaroo Jets and Jit in particular.

When Amoco Renegades won their first Panorama in 1982, however, the taste of victory awakened an appetite for new challenges, new ways to prove themselves. So they turned to the Steelband Festival competition they had only entered once before, in 1962 when it was still part of the Trinidad and Tobago Music Festival. And Jit asked Sewell to help

'For the first two festivals (1982 and 1984) Sewell would give Jit the music to teach the band and then he himself would turn up and refine the interpretation and conduct it', recalls Pat Bishop, Desperadoes' musical director and Samaroo's close friend. Sewell would recommend the music. Jit would come and arrange it. Then Sewell would refine the arrangement and take over the conducting.

They chose Strauss' 'Die Fledermaus' and Kitchener's 'Pan Explosion'. Sewell, living in faraway Point Fortin, didn't work with the band enough, they didn't practise enough, and they wanted to back out. Sewell rehearsed them over and over on the day of the competition and they entered.

It was a disaster. Some players forgot their parts and the band was eliminated in the preliminaries. But they found strength in defeat. 'For the little practice we got surprisingly high points', says Duncan. 'That was the catalyst. Men thought, if we do so good and we don't practise…'

They returned to the Festival fray in 1984 to second place with 'Orpheus in Hades' by Offenbach and 'Sweet Pan' by Kitchener. Then in 1986 their versions of Beethoven's Seventh Symphony, fourth movement, and a Michael Marcano/Jit Samaroo composition 'For the Love of Pan' did not get past the preliminaries.

By 1988 it was as if a different Renegades entered the Festival. With three Panorama titles under their belt they were accepted as a top band, and they were confident. Now other panmen were not jibing them, as in 1982, that they were not a festival band and were wasting their time. The tunes they chose to play were Kitchener's 'Pan in A Minor' and Gustav Holst's difficult 'Mars, the Bringer of War'. They had a heavy touring schedule, which did not permit enough time for rehearsals, and on the night of the competition the band was abroad. They were allowed to perform alone the following night and drew a large crowd.

They came second in the competition, and their tune of choice, 'Mars, the Bringer of War', got the highest score. Thereafter the band bowed out of the Festival circuit and has never returned, largely because their tour commitments have grown. The band's claim to fame would be earned in the Panorama arena.

Mars, the Bringer of War

I have heard almost nothing else that moved me so much – or approached the accomplishment of that night. That piece mirrored all the stories of Goldteeth, Boldface, and others. You felt a sense of their history. There was bacchanal, war, disharmony and, at some point, a kind of beauty emerges from it all. This reflected Renegades history to me. It was amazing. Sewell was able to recreate all the steelband wars of the Renegades in eight minutes of music. You could see Goldteeth cutting Melvina hand, you could see the fights between Lawbreakers and Applejackers. It was all there in the music and suddenly I saw a lot of 'badjohns', or bad whatever you like, becoming committed pannists, creating music in their own lives on the pans.

Brian Honoré

[Brian 'Commentor' Honoré is a well-known calypsonian and traditional mas performer, leader of the 'Mystery Raiders' Midnight Robbers]

The winning years

The climb had been slow and agonising but it had also been systematic, so when Renegades achieved their first 1982 Panorama victory it was no flash in the pan. In the decade of the eighties their overall Panorama achievement was superior to that of all but one or two other steelbands. In those ten years Renegades attained winner's row seven times, coming first in 1982, 1984, 1985 and 1989; second in 1981 and 1987; and third in 1980. Their indomitable spirit of perseverance, tempered in the Goldteeth years, had finally found its musical outlet. Ironically, it was under the leadership of an outsider, Patrick Penco, known in the band as Dougla for his mixture of mulatto and Indian blood ('Dougla' means bastard in Hindi).

Born and raised in middle-class Woodbrook, Dougla was drawn to Invaders as a child in the late fifties. The family moved to San Fernando for a few years, where Dougla played in his first steelband, Silver Tones. On returning to Port of Spain, he shopped around for a band to join. Invaders was too popular, too crowded.

'Then I walk about listening to bands and end up by Renegades. It wasn't that big. That was in '68', Dougla recalls. 'I listen to them play, went by a pan and start and the fellas encourage me. I end up staying there. In 1973 I was vice-captain. Fellas see the potential I had. I used to get along with everybody. I come back vice-captain in '81–'82. Then in '83 I was captain until 1990.'

Only Rudolph Charles from Desperadoes has captained a band to as many victories as Dougla. Yet when he took over, the band, having won its first Panorama in 1982, had become a victim of that success.

'After we win in '82, '83 was a trouble year, it was the lowest we ever dropped. The band wasn't together, and the captain [Randolph St Louis] had get too big. We only make the finals because we was defending champion. We didn't even make a zonal. We was 24th', says Dougla. 'When I take over the band, after the '83 Carnival, the captain he nominate me and everybody wanted to second it. To reach so high and then to drop! And we sit and decide what we doing. I get the fellas more together. During the 1980s if a man eh come to practise you go by his home and find out what happen. Communication was the success. Get together with everybody, everybody have a part to play. I used to communicate with everybody, get their views.'

It began to work. Renegades won again in 1984 and 1985. Still, there were lessons to be learnt, improvements to be made. Their performance contained yet a wrinkle of unevenness. They had been placed fifth in 1983 and 1986. A good fighter paces himself,

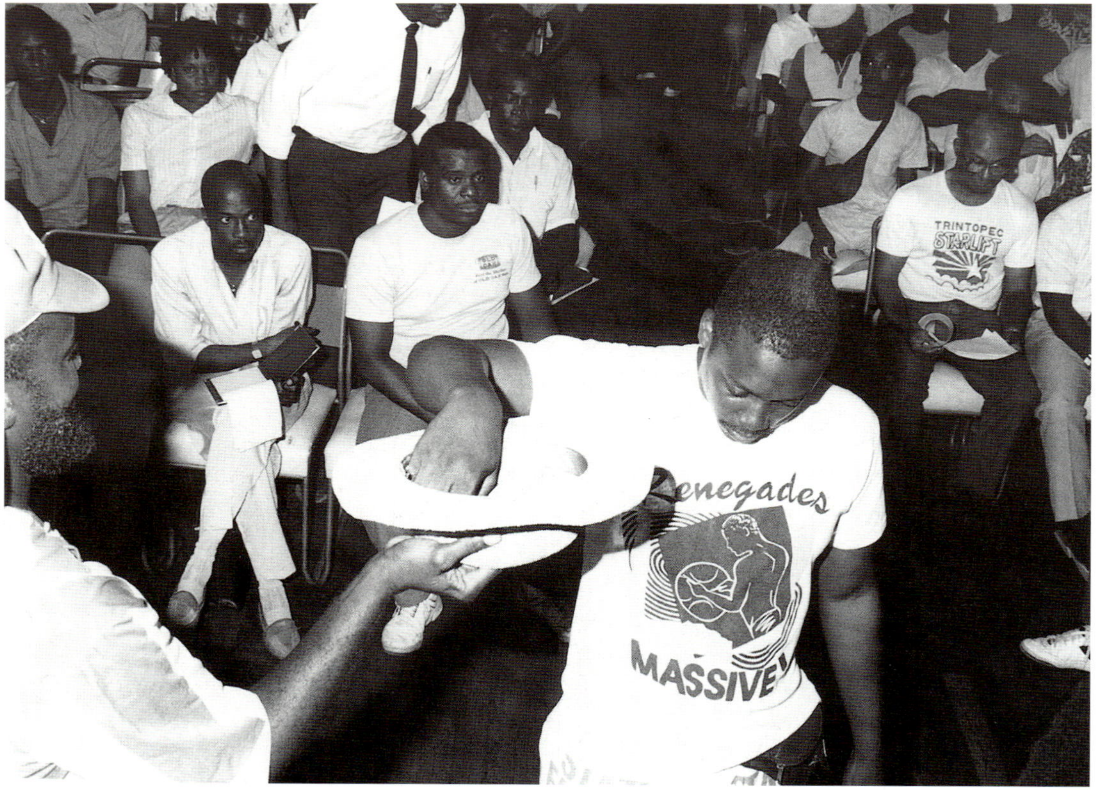

The draw for playing positions. Preliminaries, 1990. Photo courtesy of the ***Trinidad Express****.*

but on both occasions Renegades got too excited and played too fast. Then in 1988 they fell a further notch to sixth place.

'In 1988 we played "Pan in Me" and I had decided since our success was through music, we were not a jamming band, so I would emphasise music and panmanship', recalls Jit Samaroo. 'A lot was new, a three-part counter-melody, different phrases. It was rough to play but one of our best tunes up till then.' Many players thought so too, but the judges found Samaroo had not given the music a chance to breathe; it was too crowded, and the band ended up behind five other steelbands. The lesson was not lost. 'It was the first time a band played a tune without any repeats', says Duncan. 'Since that we haven't made that mistake again. We know that people like to hear things over and over, the judges too, so we give them some sweet parts over and over so they will be satisfied.'

The following two years, 1989 and 1990, the band came first. Then a decline of sorts set in, and the band came second in 1991 and third in 1992. In the wider scheme of music,

'You're supposed to train till you could do it without effort'

For Panorama you do the normal preparations: get the stands, the wheels, the pans in good repair. Then you have to get the group to practise. Sometimes it's a headache to carry on practices.

You start from October to make sure all is ready. Get the wheels checked – a trustee does that – check the stands. Call the tuner to evaluate the pans, see what needs changing. So by October you have an inventory. By January all you have to do is paint the pans and arrange practice sessions, co-ordinate the transportation and see about refreshments for the players.

We advertised for players some years ago but it wasn't because we needed players. It's just that they were too lax and we wanted to have a large crew so they'd buck up. A lot of them were perturbed. What happened is Jit counts the tune full speed. Some of them say they frustrated, they go outside and sit down. The practice grinds to a halt.

The section leaders are all stage side people. They take the music and teach it to the full yard practice. They might start with a scaled-down version: about eight or ten learn the tune and show the rest of the section leaders who will teach it to about six in the front line, about four in the second section …

The Panorama success is what put the tours on their plate. They have to sacrifice for it. You supposed to train till you could do it without effort. In the eighties it was the best years for practice. I remember we'd go to the Savannah and do the tune seven or eight times. Then you're sharp.

Andy Duncan, Amoco Renegades captain 1995–1999

TRINIDAD GUARDIAN, Thursday February 18, 1982 Page 3

All eyes tonight on pan giants

THOUSANDS will flock to the Savannah tonight to listen to what should be the cream of the nation's steelbands playing in the highly competitive semi-finals in their quest to reach the summit — the grand finals on Saturday night!

All eyes and ears will be on the ... giants of pan, particularly ... Solo, Invaders, Starlift, Rene... Deltones, Phase II, South ... etc.

And not least of a... what has been ... nonfeasance ... make th... the ... the ... thro... Hous...

SWEET RENEGADES

Charlotte St band snatches Panorama title from Phase II, Fonclaire

By FRANCIS JOSEPH

must have surprised even the composer himself. Such is the spirit of competition and competitors ... quality.

... down as one of the big surprises of ... Stars' inexplicable demise. ... smooth, sophis... Scorcher's

Renegades and Despers share Panorama honours

Three points separate ... bands

By FRANCIS JOSEPH

IT WAS bound to happen! After Thursday night's national Panorama semi-finals, when five points separated the first five bands, the final ...

Eh Fighting" and finished ninth with 271.5 points. ISCOTT Casablanca, maybe the most improved band since the preliminaries placed tenth with 269 points, with Kitchener's "Breakdance."

Trintoc Invaders must have been the most dejected band in the end, finishing 11th with 268.5 points. They played Merchant's "Pan in Danger." This band had topped the North... but fell away ...

RENEGADES REIGNS

...and boos turn to cheers for Despers

WHEN lovers of Carnival statistics look back on 1985 they will remember that the steelband Exodus placed eighth in the finals of the Panorama competition with 452.5 points. There are many among the academics, however, who will remember that the Exodus flagman was a winner in his own right, and was one of the more dynamic contributors ...

Renegades again

... London, and ... is strong and

... it will produce ... Trinidad and ... And the judges ... never be ques-

... another NIPDEC ... 1982 Panorama

Panorama, 1989: left to right, Andy Duncan, then the band's treasurer, John Selwyn, public relations officer, Patrick Penco, captain, receive the award for the 'Most Successful Band' distributed by Pan Trinbago. Photo courtesy of Frank Arlen. Newspapers headings, top to bottom: ***Trinidad Guardian*** *18 February 1982; 6 February 1989; 18 February 1985;* ***Trinidad Express*** *22 February 1982;* ***Trinidad Guardian*** *26 February 1990. Courtesy of the* ***Trinidad Guardian****, the* ***Trinidad Express*** *and the National Archives of Trinidad and Tobago.*

the differences between first, second and third are insignificant, but in Panorama there is only one real winning position – first. Also, the band had been hoping in 1991 to win three times in a row to complete the competition's first ever hat trick. By 1992 they seemed to be moving further away from winner's row. Kitchener complained publicly and bitterly that the band had been cheated, and so too did the *Trinidad Guardian* newspaper, displaying a surprising partisanship. On the other side was calypsonian David Rudder. His sympathies were with the 1992 winner – Exodus steelband, which had performed one of his calypsoes – and he penned what is perhaps the most poetic calypso about steelbands in war, his triumphant war-cry 'Dus in Yuh face'. There he alludes to both the winner's name, Exodus, and the clouds of dust churned up by steelbands at the Panorama venue.

Renegades worked harder the following year, spent longer hours drilling, and in 1993 they climbed back to the peak. Then they won again in 1995, and in 1996. Once again the hat trick was within reach, and when they won in 1997 it was to consummate a double victory: three in a row but also, with 9 firsts, a higher total of Panorama trophies than any other steelband. In 1999, Desperadoes won Panorama for the ninth-time, catching up with Renegades, and in 2000 another Desperadoes victory put the Laventille band in the lead.

'Those years we were up against formidable opponents, bands that have as good pannists and as strong organisation as us', Duncan sums up. 'It just boiled down to who was more hungry on the particular night.'

On the road, Carnival Tuesday, 1994. Photo by Arthur Edwards.

Good, better and best, however, are often decided by taste, which changes. The recent years have brought out a profound longing for an earlier, simpler time, the golden years of Creole society, when Kitchener and Sparrow produced the greatest and most danceable calypsoes ever heard, when the beat of the steelband pervaded everywhere with a slow sensuousness, and everyone, it seems, was in love. Renegades is out of synch with that pastoral sensibility, and the band's placing has fallen. Arranger Clive Bradley won the 1999 Panorama with a small country band, Nu Tones, whose mellowness harked back to the early sixties, when bossa nova was the most romantic music around. In 2000 Bradley returned to his original steelband, Desperadoes, and took them to first place that year and the one after. Meanwhile, Renegades' position slipped to 4th, 5th and 7th place.

Barring catastrophe it is unlikely the band will ever fall outside the top ten and the Trinidadian preoccupation with placing first in a musical performance seems like much ado about nothing. But it illustrates the defining role of Panorama. The Samba Schools in the Rio Carnival are little different. Ever since the seventies, steelband arrangements have been too intricate for dancing, in a way similar to how jazz became complex in the bebop era. Steelbands were too cumbersome to play on the roads for

When you see we come down
Tell them war declare in town.
Dus in their face.
Guns will be blasting for sure
In this musical war.
Dus in their face.
We looking for fight
It's trouble tonight
We feeling alright,
It's a panman war.
We come out for war
To settle the score
The tenors sawed off.
...
All Stars, Desperadoes and Renegades
Quiet, but they sharpening their music blades,
Fonclaire, the Phase and the Humming Bird,
Waiting for the judges to give the word.
And Lincoln and Bertie and Birdie and company
They love the bacchanal.
Them whe tune the pans
Now they watching the jam
In this pannist Carnival.

(David Rudder 'Dus in Yuh face')
Courtesy of David Rudder

Carnival. Accordingly, the massive public enthusiasm for the bands and their music became akin to the passion people experience at sporting events: Panorama was to the steelband movement what the World Cup is to football, Wimbledon to tennis, and the NBA finals to basketball.

Apart from the glory and, not to be sneezed at, the prize money gained from a

Panorama finals, 1997. Photo by Arthur Edwards.

Panorama victory, the winner in this steelband Olympiad is also rewarded with foreign tours. Pleasure and profit combine as its members earn money and share in their band's celebrity. Recruits are attracted and the band can pick and choose the most talented panmen from among them. The sponsors, touched by the band's prestige, feel satisfied their money has been well spent. As for the public, in Trinidad and Tobago as everywhere else, everyone loves a winner, and what more can a band as orphaned in its childhood as was Renegades possibly want?

When Amoco Renegades celebrated their victory in 1996 they could look back to almost two decades of exceptional achievement since they ranked third in 1980. It had taken them many years to get there but from that point there was no turning back and they have figured invariably among the handful of bands that dominated the competition.

1980	Jean the Netball Queen	Kitchener	3rd
1981	More Pan	Kitchener	2nd
1982	Pan Explosion	Kitchener	1st
1983	50 Years of Steel	Kitchener	5th
1984	Sweet Pan	Kitchener	1st
1985	Pan Night and Day	Kitchener	1st
1986	Pan Here to Stay	Kitchener	5th
1987	Pan in A Minor	Kitchener	2th
1988	The Pan in Me	Kitchener	6th
1989	Somebody	Devine	1st
1990	Iron Man	Kitchener	1st
1991	Rant and Rave	Tambu	2nd
1992	The Bees Melody	Kitchener	3rd
1993	Mystery Band	Kitchener	1st
1994	Pan Earthquake	Kitchener	3rd
1995	4 Lara 4	De Fosto	1st
1996	Pan in a Rage	De Fosto	1st
1997	Guitar Pan	Kitchener	1st
1998	Pan for Carnival	Shanaqua	4th
1999	Toco Band	Kitchener	5th
2000	Jump for Joy	Superblue	4th
2001	The Sound of the Ghost	Kernel Roberts	7th

Panyard view. Photo by Norman Magden, 1997.

Cityscape with panyard in foreground. 1997.

Anthony Crichlow on the triple cello. 1997.

The making of a Panorama tune

A Panorama arrangement is not created in the solitude of the arranger's head. Rather, it is architecturally constructed, piece by piece, in the panyard. The process involves the entire band, which must be taught to play the arrangement as it is being composed, and in so doing modifies it. The section leaders are taught by the arranger. They in turn pass it on to the rank and file, who practise it on their own time. Sections of the band may be drilled independently or together. Parts of the tune are repeated over and over until the players' co-ordination is perfect. Journalist Marcia Henville, herself a player for Trinidad All Stars, describes how Jit Samaroo and the Renegades did this in 1996 with De Fosto's 'Pan in a Rage'.

Photo 1999.

Monday 15 January

The short Rasta in the burgundy jeans is before the mighty Renegades steel orchestra, 'conducting'.

The background section, basses in racks arrayed across the width of the panyard, is being drilled. The pannists have just learnt a new part of this year's arrangement of De Fosto's 'Pan in a Rage', and they are running it over and over again.

It is Panorama season, when nights standing behind your pan are long and tiring, and by 1 a.m. your head tells you it cannot absorb any more music.

You feel cold on a warm evening because you want to sleep and you have to go to work in the morning but the cause just won't let you leave. If you do, you will probably have to answer to the section leader or the captain on the next day. Panmen and women have been banned from playing for that.

You are in the panyard of Renegades, the reigning Panorama champion, and the masters of steel are preparing for the battle in the Big Yard on February 4.

That is the day of the Panorama preliminary round and the zonal final. The band started practising on January 3, when members and prospective members gathered for a meeting with the committee.

It was time for laying down the law. Bandleader Andy Duncan told the assembled pannists that he wanted a 'cohesive force to battle with united armies' in the Savannah. He expected punctuality, total co-operation and dedication. They were to be in the yard promptly at 7.30, earlier if possible. The arranger, Jit Samaroo, was to meet them there and not the other way around.

They would get refreshments and money to go home. All they had to do was to commit themselves to the task in hand.

The bright, overhead lights in the panyard illuminate everything they cast their glare on – the chrome of the frontline pans and the frown on some of the faces of the guitar and cello players who cannot quite get the new part.

The rhythm men on drums, timbales, cowbell and scratchers, keep a steady soca beat, slow and easy. The pace helps to make your wrist supple and everyone comfortable with the music and the position of their instruments.

The background pans repeat the new part they have learnt. The drummer strikes four on the foot bass and they take it again from the top.

The piece is not difficult, but the phrasing is a little tricky and some are having problems.

Samaroo has given the frontline pans a descending chromatic run [musical scale proceeding by semitones] to play.

That's the easy part. The hard part is that he expects them to play it three notes at a time, the right hand striking one note, the left hand striking the other note and then back to the right hand striking the first note again. These notes have to be played on the down beat of each beat of the bar. At 60 or 70 beats per minute it is a challenge. At 120 bpms – Renegades won't play much below that – only crackshots will make it. Already one tenor is a note or two behind and the tempo has not been stepped up yet.

Photo by Pablo Delano, 1997.

Samaroo laughs when you mention it to him. 'My job is to give them the music,' he replies. 'Their job is to play it.' It sounds harsh but he knows his players. He has been arranging for Renegades for 25 years and he and his team represent a formidable combination.

He hasn't yet got to the bridge, that vital turning point in a Panorama tune. But already he is contemplating changing key from A flat, the tune's dominant key. He is not sure what he will go into. It all depends on the pans that he will work it with.

AMOCO
AMOCO

The crackshots, the frontline men on the tenors and the double seconds. Their lines can be as rapid as a bebop saxophonist, but the sustained notes are rolled even faster. Tenors generally have 28 notes – about the same as a flute. Double tenors, the choice of solo virtuosos, have 33 notes and carry the band's main melody in the highest register. First and second from left, tenor players Robert Alleyne and Rory Aleong. Photo by Pablo Delano, 1997.

His task is complex. It's all about trial and error. He could spend a whole evening in the yard, giving his players five or ten bars of music, only to scrap the whole thing the next night. It's all part of the process and panmen and women have learnt to expect it.

In the shed where they stored the pans, Aldwin Williams, a shift worker with Carib Brewery, is practising furiously by himself. He's trying to catch up with the rest of the band because he only started two days ago. If he could practise at his leisure, it wouldn't be so bad, but he is on shift now so his time is limited.

Williams has been playing pan for 28 years, 18 of them with Renegades. By the flick of his wrist and the confidence with which he plays, you know that he will catch up.

Dr Rat, a celebrity in these parts, is entertaining a female friend near the bar. Early in the afternoon, while Charlotte Street bustled with traffic, Dr Rat was in the yard painting the racks white. That is his job. Now he's relaxing, beer in hand, listening to his band.

Monday 22 January

It is 13 days away from the beginning of the battle royal. Players who are already in the panyard are going through their tune alone or in groups, running over the new music because it is easy to forget you ever learnt a part when you've had to cram notes into your head.

The middle section – cellos, guitars, quadrophonics – are learning a long solo; so too are a few tenors, the rest of whom will arrive later.

The basses have not yet been given their solo and the seconds have already learnt theirs. Some seconds players are sitting on the bottom of their racks, bored.

The double-tenor players, whose pans are principally used for harmonising, are learning snippets of the solo from the middle pans. They will do the same with the other sections.

The introduction of these solos means that Renegades is following its tried and trusted formula: long runs – scales – and arpeggios dominating the tune, snaking their way through the frontline pans, then along the middle and background pans, smooth and mellifluous.

You can expect the engine room to be a force of its own – the drummer crashing and dropping, phrasing perfectly; the iron men levelling their iron beaters at the gleaming

Photo by Pablo Delano, 2000.

silver metal, hypnotic rhythm and flair; the scratchers sizzling; the tambourines jingling and jungling; the cowbells tock-tocking like a metronome; the congas moaning rhythmically, entrancing you; and the timbales exploding at intervals.

Because Jit teaches players their solos first, before he does any bridging, it is difficult to deduce where he has reached in the tune. What you do know is that his arrangement will be classical in parts, Latin in others.

The key will change once, maybe twice, into the minor. There will be a lot of drama in keeping with the rage of 'Pan in a Rage', and there must be a jam towards the end, followed by a return to the verse and chorus. The introduction, which they will learn last of all, will be a synopsis of what the tune is about.

It's a formula that Renegades has used over and over again and which has been highly successful so far. Jit knows what the judges want.

Over on the wooden bleachers, directly in front the racks, people are liming, talking animatedly, their beer bottles standing next to them. Or they are sitting alone or in twos, soaking up Samaroo's arrangement. Some tourists arrive – they tend to be attracted to Renegades – and ensconce themselves in the bleachers too. Children are crawling all over the stanchions and one boy squares up to fight another.

Friday 26 January

Nine days are left in the countdown. Jit still hasn't bridged many of the parts and the band still has approximately three to five minutes of music to learn.

This is uncharacteristic of him, remarks one of the players. They usually learn their Panorama tune with time to spare.

The Renegades are never less than electrifying. If you ever heard 'Sweet Pan' (1984), 'Pan in A Minor' (1987), 'Iron Man' (1990), or 'The Bees Melody' (1994), you'll understand how their music affects a listener.

It's why they have won Panorama so many times.

But learning Jit's arrangement isn't easy. The phrasing is often tricky, especially this year, and the speed awesome.

It's easy to get out of tune and it's easy to lose track of where you are. Make a mistake while playing a long run, and it can mean having to wait until the entire piece has ended before you can rejoin the band – which is what the idle ones are doing now.

But if you learn your part well enough, and your hand remembers where to go when your brain stops thinking, you can slide right in again.

At the pace some of these top bands play, your hands must slip into automatic pilot anyway and the brain just reminds you of the major parts to come.

Repairing the rack's welds. Photo by Norman Magden, 1997.

Four-cello. 1998.

Sunday 4 February

Renegades, band number 28, are on the tarmac leading to the Grandstand. It is 9.15 p.m. and the players are setting up their instruments ready to run through the tune at least two or three times before they hit the stage. The band has added to the end of the tune last night so now it is virtually unrecognisable compared to last week's version. The bridges are all in place, so too is the introduction. Six minutes of disjointed parts have become ten minutes of flowing music.

The tune is not as intricate as previous Panorama arrangements, but this is only the preliminary round. Still, Jit has a tendency not to change too much of his music between preliminary, semi-final and final rounds.

As reigning champions they are automatically in the finals. But today is not just the Panorama prelims; it is also the day of the zonal finals, and the band wants to capture the North Zone title again.

Besides, for a panman or panwoman, there's no feeling like it – the preparation for impending battle and the glory of being on that stage when the cameras and all eyes are on you. When the bell or the iron sounds once, and then there's the one ... two ... three ... four ... And the explosion of sweet pan and the engine room swinging, throbbing.

If only for ten minutes, it is your moment of glory.

Photo by Norman Magden.

On the road with Renegades

In the 1960s, when steelbands moved through the city playing music, those long caravans of instruments were enthusiastically pushed by supporters of the bands. 'Pushing pan' was a statement of belonging, a privilege and a pleasure. Journalist B.C. Pires in 1996 experienced in Renegades the last flicker of this sadly vanished practice.

Carnival Thursday night, Panorama semis, and the sound of pan fades as you leave the Savannah Track and walk through Memorial Park. People sit, stretched out, sipping from paper cups, and you realise how much quieter the Park is. Near the General Hospital you feel the air quickening. People are moving faster. A man coming up Charlotte Street looks at you, pauses and turns his head, looking back towards Oxford Street corner. Your brain interprets the sudden excitement, the burst of energy and the glint of street lamp on rack roof. Renegades are leaving the panyard.

It is four city blocks from Amoco Renegades' panyard to the Savannah, and the pans have made the same journey twice before, for prelims and for the north/east finals, but it is easier tonight because there is no traffic. Renegades are playing at position number 14, and at half past ten every

Captain Andy Duncan addresses his troops one last time before they leave the panyard. Photo by Norman Magden, 1997.

motorist who wants to go to Panorama is already at the Savannah. Gleaming silver, white and red, Renegades' pans stand in the gutter while dirty yellow-band maxi-taxis weave their way in and out, picking up passengers, making money.

The first rack you meet holds a four-pan, with only the pannist himself pushing. You take hold of the purpose-built handle at shoulder height and pull, nodding to the panman who nods back. The next rack coming up the street is a good hundred metres away. Most of the Renegades' effort is still concentrated in the panyard, in the mammoth enterprise of getting the pans into the street.

You pull the four-pan along what is either Keate Street East or Memorial Park South and, until you turn the corner and pass the National Museum, all you hear is the roll of the wheels and the breathing of the panman near you. You marvel at how well-built these things are, so that provided there are no potholes one man can pull a fully loaded six-bass rack a mile without breaking sweat. You leave the rack at the tennis court entrance and go back to help pull another pan.

More and more pans are coming around the corner to Memorial Park now, rolling silently in the dark, the pannists pushing studiously, quietly listening to the music in their heads. People in Memorial Park are looking up. You hear someone say: *Eh-eh! Renegades, Boy!* and jump to come and help.

A young man grabs hold of the front handle and steers the pan to a halt at the side of the road. This is Lopez, and this is his rack. Lopez is 24 years old and has been beating pan with Renegades for eleven years – since he was thirteen. You begin to get an idea of what commitment to pan is, how much more there is to it than pulling a pan rack on a well-paved road.

After a long time with only one or two in front of the tennis courts, pan racks are arriving in groups of three and four, like London buses. And now there are calls back and forth. Renegades' pan racks are not known by the pans they carry but by the people who lead the pans. No one asks: Where the nine-bass? The search is for individuals. Where Lyndon? Where Steve? Watch his pansticks.

At the centre of the action is a man of impossible energy. He is called only Redman, obviously with respect. He struts from one end of the street to the other at a speed you have to skip to match, calling directions to others. He is a senior member of the band and people follow his instructions unquestioningly. He bends over to lift a four-pan rack partially on to the pavement and by the time he straightens his back and heaves, two other band members are helping.

The street is one-third the width of the panyard. Redman has somehow contrived to organise the pans in it and the band is ready to jam. It is 11.30. The band isn't going to be on stage for another two to three hours.

You look around. Until the stage there is just music.

Phase II is playing immediately ahead of Renegades. They go off the stage, leaving the Savannah crowd wild. The North Stand is jumping up and down and screaming and whistling. The band starts to play and after the first few notes you realise they will be the ones to beat tonight. Some people, very few, are going wild; most are silent, some standing with their mouths open in awe. Phase II supporters, in their bright purple T-shirts, are smiling in rapture.

This is more than pan, this is a gift. Renegades come to a smashing end and there is a moment of silence before the North Stand roars its unstinting approval. Renegades supporters are dancing the pans away; the players and their fans know they have put on a winning performance and it's going to be a happy roll back to the yard. A man standing next to you looks at you.

You hear pan?

he shouts in glee.

You hear PAN?

You smile, you nod.

Yes, you hear pan.

Present and former players celebrate their 1997 victory. Andy Duncan, then captain of the band, is in the front row to the left; Everald 'Redman' Watson, nine-bass player, is seated to the right. Michael Marcano, Renegades' chairman, stands in the back row, fifth from right.

Panorama: At left, Panorama 1981, photo courtesy of the ***Trinidad Express****. Top, left to right: Caudlyn Lopez on the four-cello, Panorama finals 1997, photo by Jeffrey Chock; next two photos by Norman Magden, Panorama finals, 1997.*

Bottom, left to right: Panorama finals, 1997, photo by Norman Magden; Preliminaries 1988, photo by Lester Forde, courtesy of the ***Trinidad Guardian****; flagwoman, Preliminaries, 1998, photo by Jeffrey Chock; former stage side member Al Edwards and Panorama player Evans Friday, photos by Arthur Edwards, Panorama finals, 1997.*

Members elect the band's leadership, 1997.

Panorama semi-finals, 2001.

4

The band today

New York, 1990. Centre front, Dawn Batson, conductor on tour. Photo courtesy of Frank Arlen.

Touring

Touring means an opportunity to see another part of the world and a chance to make some money. To most of us this is particularly important since we may be unemployed, temporarily employed or just need the money. It's another opportunity to show off our talent, hoping to attract more opportunities. It makes a panman feel really important and makes the time spent in the panyard seem worthwhile because of the response received from foreign audiences, most of whom have never seen or gotten close to musical trash cans before.

***Harold Moses**, elected Renegades captain in 1999*

As late as 1979 Renegades had performed abroad only three times. The following year Invaders pioneer Carlton Blackhead invited Renegades to play in New York. (Ironically, it was Blackhead who in 1948 launched Casablanca and Renegades onto their riotous trajectory.) In the next decade the Renegades' stage side travelled abroad every year excepting 1985 and 1987. In 1990 a 45-member Renegades team was featured at Paris Bastille Day with Jean-Michel Jarre before an estimated audience of two million. They've played in Gabon, Jordan, La Reunion, Argentina, Brazil, several times in Europe and the US, and throughout the Caribbean. In the 1990s they went abroad almost three times every year. After their first trip to Japan they've been invited back repeatedly.

Success breeds success. The band's Panorama victories have made them one of the top-billing steelbands in the world, while the continuous rehearsal by the touring side has made those core Renegades players some of the most skilled pannists in Trinidad.

This core group contains all the section leaders in the band, and has moulded them into a tightly knit team, which includes its arranger and its tuner. At any one time the stage side would have a memorised repertoire of about 70 tunes.

'Working with the Jets and with Renegades – I've been with Renegades for such a long time it's almost the same. With Jets people do their own parts, I just tell them the chords and the style. And soon Renegades will be so too. Some could do it already', says Samaroo. 'My relationship with the players is the same. Renegades is like my second family. Most of those guys I've known as kids.'

It's not just the continuous practising of the stage side which has bonded the group so tightly, but the intimacy of touring together, sharing hotel rooms, long flights and bus rides, and co-ordinating the many tasks necessary for mounting a good performance in a foreign country. Even before it's decided who handles which pans, it's determined who's in charge of loading the bus. 'Everybody is seasoned now', says Samaroo. 'We don't take many new players – one or two, and that's on short trips.' For the Bastille Day concert in Paris the 45-member side had to assemble their instruments and get in

The band playing at Columbia University, 1990. Photo courtesy of Frank Arlen.

Paris, 14 July 1990. The 45-member Amoco Renegades stage side performed in the laser-show directed by pop composer and multi-media performer Jean-Michel Jarre before an estimated audience of two million. Photo by Charlotte Rampling.

position within five minutes. They rehearsed the procedure step by step to a stopwatch. On the actual night they completed it in three minutes.

'The European agent put three people on our bus to study how we operate as a group this size', recalls Samaroo. 'One was from Burundi, another from Albania. They had smaller groups but still got serious problems getting it together.'

In Renegades' favour is the discipline which has endured since the Goldteeth era in the fifties. People aren't given a clout for indiscipline as before, but slackness is not tolerated and the tour manager's report is serious business. 'If you're late they fine you. If they say dress shoes and you have the wrong shoes – fine. And they mean that', explains Samaroo. 'One New York tour was rough. We had a performance and some guys went shopping. I hear a stampede and I see a set of them running to get in one minute before the performance. We arrived one minute after – they fined everybody. One man forgot his glasses – fine. Many of them paid a lot of money on that tour.'

Such rare instances give the wrong impression, though, for touring is a joy to the members. 'It's different from the panyard, everybody's closer', says Leslie Ann Francis, who went to Paris and New York with

Paris 1993. Michael Marcano first played with several other bands before joining Renegades in 1984 as a double seconds player. Several times chairman of the band (1991–1993, 1996–1997, 2000–) he was also vice-president of Pan Trinbago (1993 to 1996) and is a manager at TSTT (Telecommunication Services of Trinidad and Tobago). Photo courtesy of Michael Marcano.

Outside a French café, 1993. Left to right, Miguel Lopez, Dexter Bernard, Andrew Brumant, Lanel Lopez, Brian Brumant, Trevor Osborne. Photo courtesy of Michael Marcano.

the team. 'When we're outside no one has any problems to worry about, everybody's more relaxed, joking on the buses, playing cards.' And when it comes to pulling together, the band functions like clockwork.

'In Argentina the function started at 8 p.m. and the band was to play at 11.30', says Amoco Public Relations Officer Frank Arlen. 'At 8 p.m. we were still in the airport.' They had to load the instruments, get to the venue, set up the band on stage. 'They'd only had about two hours sleep the night before but they held hands, said a prayer, and played for hours straight. They had people jumping and waving like crazy.'

And there is more to it than that. Musically, touring has increased the band's repertoire and sophistication, as when they had the opportunity to hear the tango played in Argentina. As part of his stint in Japan Brian Brumant has arranged Japanese music for pan. Asked in 1993 what the players had learned from a tour in Europe, Michael Marcano, the tour manager, answered: 'Professionalism and the necessity to read scores'*. The players feel part of the international music scene. The contacts with musicians and concert organisers overseas and the warm welcome with which steelband music is received in all parts of the world have enlarged their experience and vision.

They are not professionals who earn their livelihood solely from music, but the dream is there for many. Already touring is an important source of revenue for the band, and the players also get a modest stipend. Ultimately, for them, touring is like being paid to hang out with close buddies, see different places, learn new things and win new fans by doing what they best do. That is, by playing pan.

*Quoted in F.I.R. Blake, ***The Trinidad and Tobago Steelpan, History and Evolution*** *(F.I.R. Blake, 1995), p.280.*

Japan, 1994. Photo courtesy of Andy Duncan.

Brian Brumant with a Japanese Koto musician at the Central Bank Auditorium. 2000.

Brian Brumant,
tenor

As a boy I used to play on milk tins. We used to tune them and anything Renegades play we play. I was living next door in the plannings. My brother Andrew – Soca – was the drummer. He had a plastic cover on a milk tin. The metal from the top was the cymbals. That was in the early seventies. I remember the tune at the time: 'Black Skin Blue-Eyed Boy'.

Selwyn John – Snail – took us in the tent and teach us how to play. Now I'm the leader of the tenor section and my brother is the drummer. I joined the band in 1981 and I've made every tour: Japan, France, Brazil, Jamaica, Guadeloupe, Jordan, Spain, Germany, England, Canada, New York.

Japan was the place we left a mark. Toyama is a small city, about 15,000. There was a festival, Suki Yaki Meets the World: musicians came from all over to it for one week and Renegades was invited. People was crazy about us. The audience was part of the concert. We got them involved in the show, dancing on the stage.

The Japanese promoters, Conversation Company Ltd, wanted us to do some workshops in 1995, so I went to teach the basics of pan. They got it real fast and they decided to form a band, the Suki Yaki Steel Orchestra. I taught all pans, I play all. So I became their arranger.

One problem I had: Japanese people live in their culture. They stick to their music. I had to explain each piece of music, its feel, what it represents. It was tough at first because they're not accustomed to dancing so I had to be a dance tutor. Now it's easier.

I have to take it slowly. Every year I add intricacies. This year I'll do a classical piece. I like choreography, it's visual, so we'll do light works so they could create a show. The music will tell a story: where pan came from. It starts with a person pounding a pan. It's all to get more drama in it.

I also do Japanese music. It takes to pan nicely. In Japan there's a three-string guitar that sounds similar to pan. They pluck it.

Winston 'Crawl' Downes,
triple cello

I started pan in Laventille in the seventies in Music Makers up Picton Road. It was a small band and it mashed up and I was on my way to Pandemonium. I decided to take a shortcut and I passed by Renegades. I saw Jit showing somebody 'Symphony in G' on the three-cellos. I liked it and I joined the band that year. It was 1979. I played in Panorama in 1980. That year I went to Carifesta in Barbados. When you go on tour it's one big family. It's a good feeling and it brings the band closer.

Renegades' annual general meeting, 1997.

Women in the band

Once, just setting foot in a panyard might have damaged a young woman's reputation. Nowadays respectable women from all classes not only play pan but are able to go on tours or conduct steel orchestras. They have become an indispensable part of the contemporary pan scene. In 1998 a woman was elected captain of Phase II, one of Port of Spain's top bands. Even though her tenure lasted less than a year, it is a sign of the times. Women joined Renegades a little more slowly than some other steelbands but their number has steadily increased over the recent years. Obviously they are here to stay.

Tenisha John on the bass, Panorama finals, 1997. On slow tunes the bass can be the easiest pan to learn, especially basses with fewer drums, because they are not played quickly nor rolled. Accordingly, many of the first women to play pan began on the bass. To achieve virtuosity on the bass is as difficult as with any other pan, although in a different way. The speed required by a Panorama tune or some classical pieces such as Tchaikovsky's 1812 Overture isn't of the wrist but of the entire body. The player is surrounded by the instrument. Notes are in front, behind, above, and to get to them in sequence calls for elaborate footwork, spinning, reaching behind and twisting at the waist. A good bass player's movements can be as graceful and precise as any choreography.

Initially, the steelband movement was a masculine affair. The drumming traditions it grew out of, the street gangs that supported it, were a man's province. Both its orchestration and its violence enhanced a male bonding as did also respectable society's rejection. In 'Outcast', the Mighty Sparrow sang a lament for panmen but also for panwomen: 'If your sister talk to a steelband man/The family want to break she hand/Put she out, lick out every teeth in she mouth'.

Still, those early bands depended on their matriarchs and Renegades was no different. Before them, Bar 20 was nurtured by Muriel White, a well-known dresser around the dives of Port of Spain in the 1930s and a brothel-keeper in the 1940s. Muriel had waved flag for Bar 20, which was based opposite her house in Bath Street, for she had a soft heart for those outcast young men of the early steelband movement. Born in 1904, Muriel was senior to the oldest panmen, and this tall, rowdy, pipesmoking woman indulged them like the sons she didn't have, feeding them, allowing them to stay at her place when they had nowhere else to go, hiding them from the law, and this she continued through three generations of young men, starting with those in Bar 20. So it was hardly surprising when Bar 20 captain Ancil Boyce became involved with her daughter, Phyllis White.

Bar 20 dissolved after Boyce died, and Phyllis in turn adopted the band that would become the Renegades, waving its flag on the road and gambling with its young members who were friends with her only son Cecil. Dr Rat, for instance, one of the youngest early Renegades, whose son would in turn become one of their main Panorama flagmen, was close to Cecil White. 'Phyllis was older and used to beat all of we', he says, recalling the times they gambled as teenagers in the yard behind Muriel and Phyllis's house. 'She used to sit with she legs wide so, and while we studying to look under she, she looking at your hand.'

Later, when Therese 'Sackina' Edwards, who worked in Miramar nightclub where Goldteeth was the bouncer, moved in with him, she became the band's flagwoman.

Such were the females in the band in the 1950s and 1960s, women like Marlene Gill, Irma Payne, Jean 'Jean-in-town' Clarke, Brenda

'Chunks' Parson, Beryl Baptiste. Violent, hard-drinking women, at least one of them, Jean-in-town, was a prostitute. These women were not scared by the band's reputation. 'I born and grow in the Harpe and my two brothers, Papito and Axe, was in the band', says Beryl Baptiste, 53. 'I wanted to play pan but you know your mother – they was strict with girls. She'd beat you half to death if she hear you playing pan. She didn't mind me supporting the band because they was safe: if they take you out they bring you back.'

Indeed, some of the women were attracted by Renegades' notoriety, added to it even, coming out with the band on Carnival Monday in no more than the sheerest of nightdresses, as did the *jamettes* of a century before. As Muriel White says of her daughter, 'She liked all that bacchanal'.

They didn't play pan, true, but they supported the panmen to the hilt. 'Give them a knife or a gun to hold and they hold it', says Boldface, remembering the Lawbreakers era. 'If police search me I have nothing, but if a fight break out I have something.' Beryl Baptiste goes even further. 'Is we used to start the riot', she claims. 'If anything happen, is Marlene and I used to pelt the first bottle and mash up the fête. I used to tote they gun, cutlass, anything, even with my big belly.'

Candace Andrews with Jit Samaroo. 1997.

Candace Andrews, *double seconds section leader*

I was living next to the panyard. I always loved pan, would always go to Panorama. One night I went to the section I liked and told the section leaders – Sean Nero and Edmund Willis – that I liked it. They asked me if I had sticks. It was difficult on the double seconds. Fortunately I finished the whole tune. Although I was not perfect, as I'd finished they allowed me to play in the prelims. I had CXC [examinations] after so I rest three years but a friend brought pans for me and Sean would come home and help. In 1995 I started back. I don't know if it was my practice or my eagerness but I made it for all the Panorama nights and I joined the stage side that same year. In 1996 I became section leader for Panorama. My first tour to Chicago was real, real good. I did my best and from the manager's report I was a promising player. Then in 1996 I went to Japan. Then Guadeloupe. My biggest wish is to learn music theory.

Eleanor Thomas, the wife of former Renegades captain Patrick 'Dougla' Penco, was one of the earliest 'decent' women around the band, she and Cynthia Lopez, and that was in the late sixties. As young women both of them lived on Oxford Street, Lopez further up the street, Thomas right opposite the pan tent. 'When I start waving flag for them my father was vex but I didn't bother with him. Every year they would come and beat for Mama and Daddy and when they win he give them 25 cases of beer', says Thomas. 'All my friends used to say, "How you go with Renegades?" but them badjohn fellas used to take care of you, nobody cyar interfere with you when you in the band.'

For her part Lopez was more circumspect, and not because of the badjohns. 'It was real bad girls in the band', she says. 'I didn't play mas with them because of that, I just went to hear them because my husband was in the band.' Nevertheless, she eventually became the band's cook, feeding them at late-night Panorama rehearsals, selling pies in the pan theatre during practice sessions, and has for the past eight years carried their banner.

Today hardly a dozen women play with the band for Panorama, about 10 per cent of the full team – a minuscule figure compared to most other top steelbands. But whereas some bands have had female players since the 1950s and even the 1940s, Renegades' reputation kept female pannists out until the late 1980s. Even then the first weren't from the immediate neighbourhood but from Belmont, whose steelbands Pandemonium and Casablanca were in decline. Bassist and secretary Kathy Ann Sample, for instance, comes from Belmont and joined Renegades in 1987.

Although the band is behind the times, Sample represents a general trend whereby young recruits come from the secondary school bands with which they have some connection. She first attended Belmont Junior Secondary School, whose steelband was tutored by a Renegades member, and then she went to South East Port of Spain Secondary School whose band used Renegades instruments. Similarly three-cello player Dawn Songster, Renegades secretary for five years, also comes from Belmont, also attended those two schools and joined the band in 1986. 'By then', she says, 'they were more known and had won three Panoramas.' The following year bassist Leslie-Ann Francis, from the same neighbourhood and school, joined. Karen Granderson, however, tried Pandemonium and Casablanca before coming to Renegades in 1991. It was now easy for double seconds section leader Candace Andrews, who lived next to the panyard, to just take the plunge and join.

These women all attended co-educational schools, as did the men they play alongside, and they are comfortable together. Their proportion will certainly even out. But for women one day to dominate steelbands as they now dominate the academic sphere, they would need to spend endless hours with their band, an independence their domestic commitments still don't allow wives and mothers. In such an event they would become, in every sense, Renegades.

Band members in a vacant lot along Basilon Street, by where the band began. Left to right: Rudolf Grant, six-tenor bass; Obasi Farai, tenor; Leslie Ann Francis, four-tenor bass; Edsel Joseph, tenor; Anna Rodney, double seconds; Edward Nicholas, double guitar; Dexter Bernard, double tenor; Beverly Gomez-Brown, three-cello. 1997.

RENEGADES
Amoco Renegades
MECCA

SNAIL
Renegades
adidas
AMERICA
PERRY ELLIS
Greetings
AMOCO
Renegades
AMOCO
RENEGADES
AMOCO
Renegades

Looking ahead

Today, pan is global. It embraces and has been embraced by cultures all over the world. You can find steelbands from Argentina to Alaska, from Japan to Jamaica. The Dutch police have one, so too does the Nigerian army.

Trinidad remains the heartland, but not as before. Youth culture has drifted away and every band's community has shrunk. A new member can no longer learn pan tunes merely by hanging around and looking on. New reservoirs of talent must be found and tapped with new incentives. These challenges to a band's survival are novel. So are the opportunities it can seize.

Front row, from left to right: Selwyn 'Snail' John, tenor; Robert Alleyne, tenor; Dexter Bernard, double tenor; Allison Sample, tenor; Obasi Farai, tenor; Karen Granderson, tenor; Leslie-Ann Francis, bass; Anselm Gibbs, bass; Errol 'Ras' Begg, tenor.

The Renegades story is the matter of fairy tales. It is the ugly duckling that became a swan, the Cinderella that turned into a princess. Only it was not just the good luck of finding a prince to kiss the frog and make the transformation. It took hard work and persistence, and a will, a deep-seated longing to win.

Pass along Oxford Street during a weekday between half seven and half nine at night. You'll hear music from the Renegades pan theatre, the home where members have signed their names on the walls. If some competition or a tour is imminent, the sessions will go later, rehearsal will be more systematic. The arranger will be there. The captain too, often chiding latecomers. But even if the band is abroad, there will still be a few young men and women in the small rectangular shed practising, practising and practising. To their right stands a blackboard on which is chalked the 50 or 60 tunes they must know by heart.

None of this work is paid but that is what it takes, a commitment to spend four out of seven nights drilling, and that is out of the Panorama season. In January and February it is six out of seven nights in the panyard. Then a night can go past midnight.

Generally, only young people can sustain such commitment. Dedication, commitment, discipline, the words only skirt the issue; what is required is love.

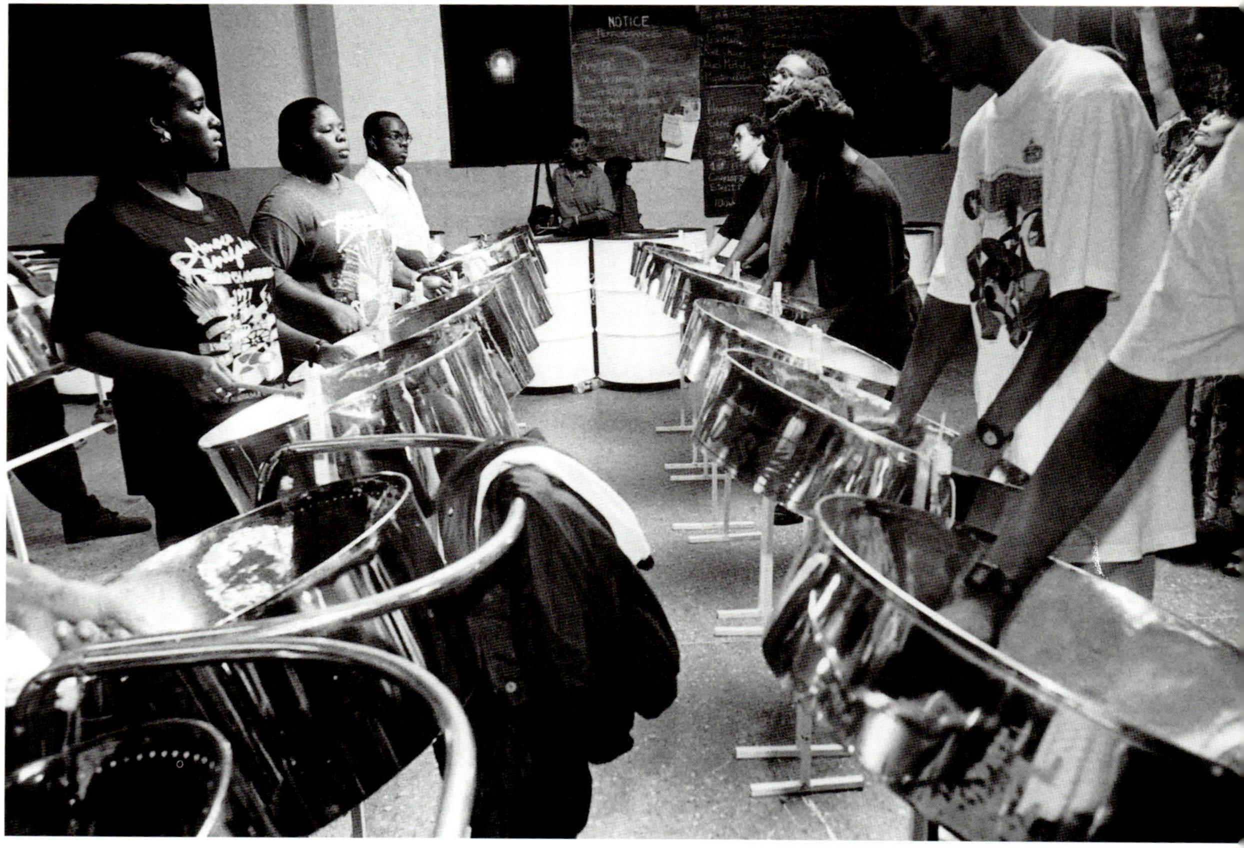

In the pan theatre. From left to right: Anna Rodney, double seconds; Candace Andrews, double seconds; Sean Nero, double seconds; Leslie Ann Francis, four-tenor bass; Karen Granderson, tenor; Allison Sample tenor; Errol 'Ras' Begg, tenor; Obasi Farai, tenor. 1997.

It was a love of heroic dimensions that impelled a generation of working-class men to sustain the organisations which fostered the invention of the instrument. They fought against society and against one another. Today steelbands are no longer comprised of angry young men. From being outlaws they are now the pride of the nation, and in this sense the Renegades story is that of the steelband movement writ small.

Making of itself one of the greatest competitive steelbands ever, the Renegades Steel Orchestra had to evolve into a very different organisation from what it once was. Just as the shift from Basilon Street to La Cour Harpe in 1963, and the election of Lawbreaker Ossie McSween, was symbolic of what they became in the sixties, so too the

1977 move to the Charlotte Street panyard – and the election of Andy Duncan, a prison officer, to the position of trustee – was also significant.

Times have changed. You don't find the simple intimacy of the fifties and the sixties. Administration is a more formal bureaucracy. Since the sixties the band has had a relatively large executive group, but even so all members pulled their weight in a sort of *ad hoc* fashion. Nowadays, the band's executive functions are very specific to certain offices. There is a captain of the band, a chairman of the organisation, a secretary, an assistant secretary, a treasurer, two trustees, two floor representatives, a public relation officer and a senior members' representative.

In the 1960s the band had no more than a dozen regular players, maybe sixty for Panorama. Today BP Renegades has a much larger membership. In addition to the band, which in the Panorama season swells to around two hundred playing members, the organisation has nearly another two hundred financial members. The stage side alone comprises about forty semi-professional players. The panyard on Charlotte Street, visited by large crowds every night in the Carnival season, is one of the country's poshest.

Success has made the band a favourite of the general public. Renegades T-shirts are worn with pride by people of every race and class from every part of the country. And the players themselves display the self-confidence of winners. But the BP Renegades of today still has much of the personality it forged 35 years ago. The band shows the same combativeness of the rioting days, only now it is sublimated into the Panorama competition. The early emphasis on discipline is still there, and perhaps a certain they-don't-really-like-us defensiveness. This collective rigour is one reason for their Panorama achievements, for it has honed their orchestration to a faultless precision, enabling them to execute Jit Samaroo's difficult music exactly as he conceived it. It is also what makes their touring side function so efficiently that it could impress even the Japanese.

Brandt Speede-Waldron, Dexter Bernard, Eagan Trotman, repair a damaged panstick. 1997.

This is necessarily at the expense of the individual, and consequently Renegades players don't stand out as virtuosos, even when they are indeed very good pannists. The culture of the organisation, its personality, flows in the opposite direction. This began in the early years when the band had to survive without any panmen who had outstanding musical charisma.

Beyond discipline, continuity with the past may well be the most salient characteristic of the Renegades, and the main reason

Children at the 1997 General Annual Meeting. The boy with the baseball cap is the son of bassists Leslie Ann Francis and Lanel Lopez, himself the nephew of John Lopez, a Renegades member since the late 60s. Lanel's two brothers, Miguel and Caudlyn, also play in the band. Such a case is not unique. More than a third of the present members of the stage side joined the band as sons, brothers or nephews of older family members. Photo 1997.

behind their success. They are the only band to have had the same sponsor, arranger and tuner for over two and a half decades. The last joined in the sixties, and although players are younger than executive members, and a significant number of them came into the band during the 1990s, the stage side is also a rock of tradition. Some players go back to the early seventies.

The bond between the players, their sense of belonging, is still strong, and is reinforced by the number of players who still come from the same neighbourhoods east of the Dry River within two or three miles' radius. 'In the earlier days, a number of us used to lime together a lot, practise day and night, liming, practising. We try to maintain this, being like a family', says one player. But the cultural environment has changed. In the 1980s the best players from the Panorama side were drafted into the stage side. Today, the gap between the Panorama side and the stage side is far wider. It is not only that the stage side now has about a hundred tunes; the players' motivations are different.

'I came into the band for the love of it', says Miguel Lopez, who joined in the 1980s. 'I just loved playing and being part of the band. Today this is not enough. You don't have people playing pan just for the love of it any more. They want to know there is a future. A lot of people, they want to play but they also come to the band because they know we travel a lot. When they discover how much work it takes, they drop out. If they saw a future, if they could earn money, they would stay.'

A steelband is a community of concentric circles, starting with the inner stage side core, then expanding through the senior administrative members, the large Panorama side, long-standing partisans and pioneers, neighbourhood sympathisers and, finally, the fickle public. When steelbands were mobile, rhythm integrated these circles. An itinerant band bore its community along with its music. That is no more. Steelbands no longer take to the streets like an army on the march; rather, a few players may be ferried on the back of a truck. Besides, their

Captain (1995–1999)

Renegades is the only band I was ever in. My first stint in administration was on the disciplinary committee under Boldface, 1969. I played bass. Then I played tenor, double tenor, then quadrophonic – that's the last pan I played.

I got on the executive as a trustee about 1980. Then I was treasurer, then captain. It's a lot of hard work and frustration, though when you're at our stage, it's not difficult.

Renegades has eleven officers: a chairman, captain, secretary, assistant secretary, treasurer, two trustees, two floor representatives, a public relations officer and a senior members' representative. We always had a big executive. The senior members' representative came in 1989.

The band and the organisation are different. Though the organisation revolves around the band, that's just one component. The yard has to be managed. The chairman is the man responsible for developing the yard, a plan to have it functional. He's the main man, though he may have people appointed to come up with ideas. I have my responsibility to see the band equipped, cut all gigs, hold practice. The PRO will see about gigs, he'll see about making the band known to people who have an interest in having steelband music.

We have no manager. We use people from the executive committee to manage the organisation. They are responsible for interfacing with promoters, players' problems, ensuring contractual obligations are met, everything. The captain on tour, he'll have those functions but I've taken a position: other people contribute and ought to get a chance to tour.

We built the band in the seventies, building the organisation so that the guys who now enjoy the benefit have a solid base to launch from. We had a nice rapport with arranger, tuner and sponsor. That is one of the dynamic structures. The present-day band is built on it.

Andy Duncan

Former captain Andy Duncan (1995–1999) shows the author and editors archives documenting Renegades' history.

Harold Moses, captain, on the four cello. 2000.

music is too melodic. When a group needs to sustain its cohesion, a demonstration, for instance, or an excursion, drums are used, and iron. And even that does not appeal to a television generation whose musical tastes draw them more to boom boxes blasting Jamaican dancehall and American rap.

In this environment the problem is to find a reservoir of new blood. Not just good players, but young people willing to devote the considerable amount of time and effort necessary to keep the organisation vibrant. In response the band has formed a junior group of fifty members, all under nineteen years old. Although they are drawn from all over Port of Spain, half of them come from the neighbourhood or nearby. Hopefully some of those who pass through the programme will graduate to the stage side. Initially, however, that youth group comprises its own self-contained steelband. Samaroo arranges for them and they are given music lessons twice weekly by his old teacher Fitzroy Gadjar.

'We expect them to be more trained than we were, even doing sightreading of music', says captain Harold Moses. 'Now even the senior members of the stage side can't sightread, but we want them to become true professional musicians who could read and write scores.'

Many of the players indeed seem to agree that music literacy is the key to a professional future. Not that they need to read music to play with the band; they can memorise the tunes as pannists have always done. But if they want to play with other musical ensembles, on an individual basis or as a group when the band travels abroad, they need to be able to read scores and be musically trained. As Simeon Sandiford, who has recorded Renegades' Panorama music since the 1990s, predicts: 'They have good agencies looking after booking. They can perform with international artists. Once they become proficient in music, many doors will open.'

Other plans are afoot to increase the band's self-sufficiency and generate income for its members. They entail expanding the pan theatre to include a small concert hall,

Point Fortin Borough Day, 2001.

and opening a restaurant and small shops, including a Renegades gift shop. This ambitious plan is very much in the tradition of the steelband movement whose bands have historically embraced welfare commitments to their members. Goldteeth, Desmond Baird, George Beckles and others dipped into their own pockets to assist the band's unemployed younger members.

If these projects are realised, they will certainly ensure that the BP Renegades remain a top steelband and a successful organisation. Will it preserve the hunger for success that made them the greatest? 'We believed that the limits other people set for you, you don't have to accept them', says former captain Andy Duncan. 'Hopefully that will prevail.'

Behind the bridge. The pan theatre (forefront, at right) with its entrance on Oxford Street.

Bibliography

Anthony, Michael: *Parade of the Carnivals of Trinidad, 1839–1989.* Circle Press, Port of Spain, 1989.

Beckles, George: 'East Port of Spain Youth Movement', in *Report on Central East Port of Spain Youth Centre.* n.p., 1966.

Blake, F.I.R.: *The Trinidad and Tobago Steelpan, History and Evolution.* F.I.R. Blake, Port of Spain, 1995.

Brereton, Bridget: *Race Relations in Colonial Trinidad, 1870–1900.* Cambridge University Press, Cambridge, 1979.

Cowley, John: *Carnival, Canboulay and Calypso.* Cambridge University Press, Cambridge, 1996.

Elder, Jacob D.: *From Congo Drum to Steelband: A Socio-historical Account of the Emergence and Evolution of the Trinidad Steel Orchestra.* University of the West Indies, St Augustine, Trinidad, 1969.

Goddard, George 'Sonny': *Forty Years in the Steelbands, 1939–1979.* Karia Press, London, 1991.

Grant, Cy: *Ring of Steel; Pan Sound and Symbol.* Macmillan Educational, London, 1999.

Hill, Donald R.: *Calypso, Callaloo: Early Carnival Music in Trinidad.* University Press of Florida, Gainesville FL, 1993.

Hill, Errol: *The Trinidad Carnival, Mandate for a National Theatre.* University of Texas Press, Austin and London, 1972. Re-released Beacon Press, London, 1997.

Howe, Darcus and Bukka Rennie: 'The Unemployed and the Special Works', in Susan Craig (ed.): *Contemporary Caribbean: A Sociological Reader*, Vol. 2, n.p., 1982, pp.127–36.

Johnson, Kim: 'Body Music to Sweet Pan', Sunday supplement of the *Trinidad Express* (5 instalments), Trinidad, 17 January–21 February 1993; 'Pan Pioneers', id., (30 instalments), 22 December 1996–20 July 1997 and January and March 1998; 'Notes on Pan', *The Drama Review*, Trinidad and Tobago Carnival issue, ed. Milla Riggio, Fall 1998 (T159) pp.60–73.

Kronman, Ulf: *Steel Pan Tuning: A Handbook of Steel Pan Making and Tuning.* Musikmuseet, Stockholm, 1991. Available on the internet: www.musikmuseet.se/pan/tuning/

Lovelace, Earl: *The Dragon Can't Dance.* Faber, London, 1998.

Manette, Ellie: 'The Story of Pan', *The Sun*, Trinidad, 21 March–16 May 1986 (nine weekly instalments).

Maxime, Gideon: *Pan through the Years 1952–1996.* Gideon Maxime, Port of Spain, n.d.

Pierre, Lennox: 'From Dustbins to Classics', Independence supplement of the *Trinidad Guardian*, 26 August 1962, pp.107–10.

Prospect, G.A.: *Treatise on the Steelbands of Trinidad and Tobago.* G.A. Prospect, Port of Spain, 1970.

Rohlehr, Gordon: *Calypso and Society in Pre-Independence Trinidad.* Gordon Rohlehr, Port of Spain, 1990.

Sealey, J. and K. Malm: *Music in the Caribbean.* Hodder & Stoughton, London, 1982.

Seon, Donald: *South Panmen.* Donald Seon, San Fernando, 1979.

Stuempfle, Stephen: *The Steelband Movement, The Forging of a National Art In Trinidad And Tobago.* University of the West Indies Press, Barbados, 1995.

Thomas, Jeffrey (ed.): *Forty Years of Steel: An Annotated Discography of Steel Band and Pan Recordings, 1951–1991.* Greenwood Press, Westport CN and London, 1992.

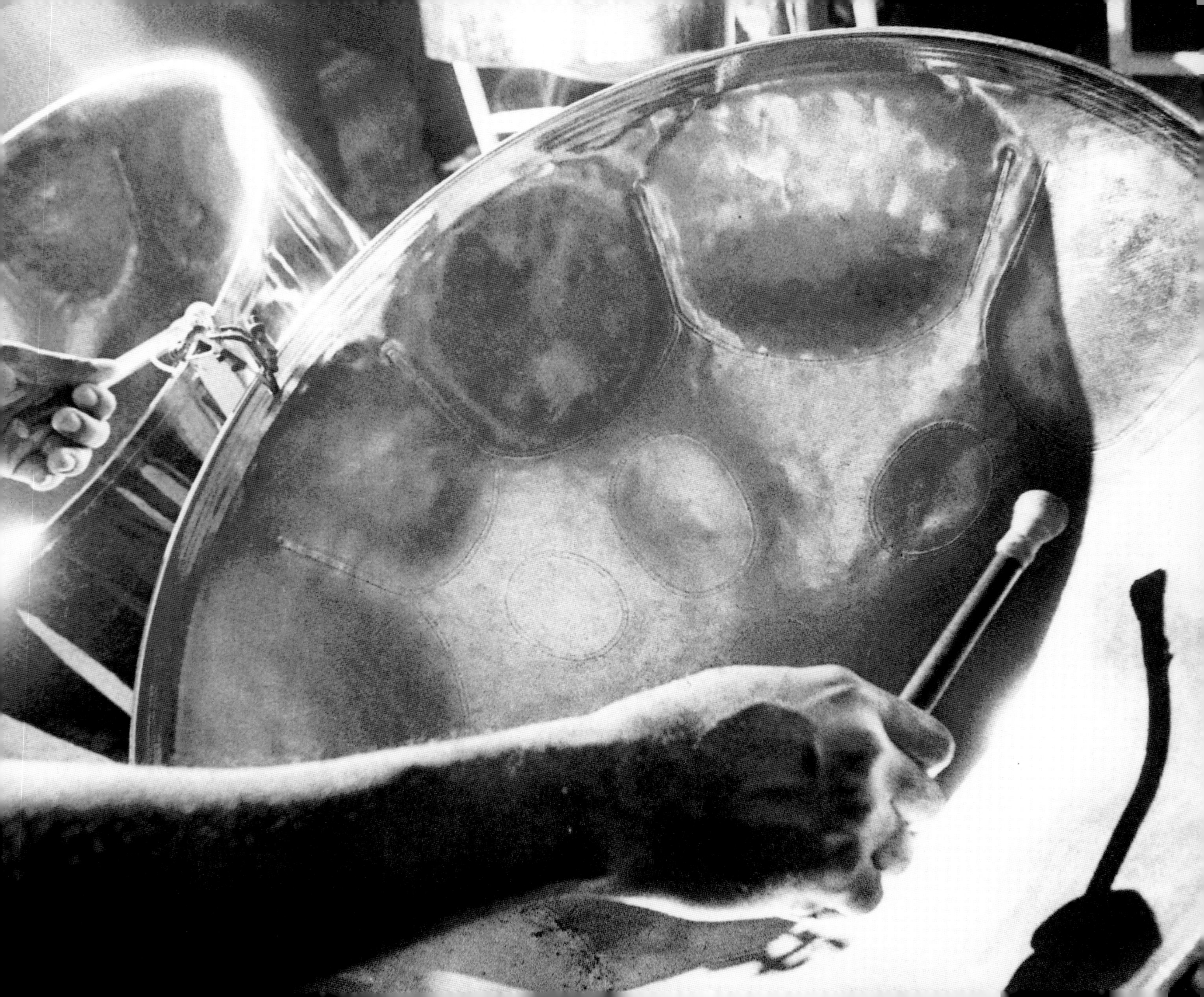

Index